How to Write a Logline

Quick Guidebook for Screenwriters

Dr. Melissa Caudle

PUBLISHER

PUBLISHING HOUSE

www.opendoorpublishers.com
Publisher since 2005

www.onthelotproductions.com

 is registered trademarks of On the Lot Productions, LLC (Logo created by Melanie Bledsoe)

Copyright ©2011 by Dr. Melissa C Caudle
All Rights Reserved

ISBN-13: 978-1467993111
ISBN-10: 1467993115

Cover and interior designs: Dr. Melissa Caudle
Cover filmstrip photograph credits: Photography Credits in the Appendix
Copy proof editor: Robby Cook Stroud

Graphic logos and designs: On the Lot Productions, LLC and are Copyright Protected

Author Picture by Tim Moree
Introduction montage design: On the Lot Productions, LLC – Individual Photo Credits Listed in the Appendix
Chapter 1 photo: On the Lot Productions, LLC – Blood Splatter by Simon Howden
Chapter 2 photo: On the Lot Productions, LLC – Blood Splatter by Simon Howden
Chapter 3 photo: On the Lot Productions, LLC – Individual Photo Credits Listed in the Appendix
Chapter 4 photo: On the Lot Productions, LLC – Individual Photo Credits Listed in the Appendix
Chapter 5 photo: Kelly Peterson
Chapter 6 photo: Simon Howden
Chapter 7 photo: Simon Howden

All photos in the book used with the permission of their copyright owners and/or www.freedigitalphotos.net

54321

HOW TO WRITE LOGLINE

Quick Guidebook for Screenwriters

By

Dr. Melissa Caudle

www.opendoorpublishinghouse.com

DISCLAIMER

Dr. Melissa Caudle, On the Lot Productions, LLC, nor Open Door Publishing House cannot guaruntee that by following the information in this book your screenplay, or film, will get green light or be accepted by television networks or production studios as a result of writing your logline.

This book was written for educational purposes only and not as legal, tax, or accounting advice. We cannot be responsible for any documents or loglines you create as a result of this book. We cannot take any responsible with what the reader does with the informaiton we provide and any documents the reader produces should be reviewed by a qualified entertainment attorney in the state in which you live. Each state has unique laws.

Likewise, only an attorney can give legal advice and only an accountant can give financial advice. When dealing with the entertainment industry, always seek professional advice. Likewise, always register your completed work, film, screenplay, treatment, synopis, and logline with either the Writer's Guild of America (WGA) or the U.S. Library of Congress.

On the Lot Productions, LLC nor Dr. Melissa Caudle accepts unsolicted scripts, screenplays, business plans, or reality show projects. For information on how to submit your project visit www.onthelotproductions.com.

Register for a free newsletter at www.therealityofrealitytv.com for the latest information on screenwriting and creating reality shows by Dr. Melissa Caudle.

TABLE OF CONTENTS

ACKNOWLEDGEMENT III

SPECIAL THANKS V

DEDICATION VI

INTRODUCTION 1

   THE MILLION-DOLLAR HOOK 1

   ABOUT THE BOOK 2

   WHAT ORDER TO PURCHASE THE FOUR BOOKS 5

   HOW TO USE THIS BOOK 6

CHAPTER ONE 7

LOGLINES: THE HOOK 7

   WHAT IS A LOGLINE? 7

      Defining the Subject 9

      Defining the Verb 11

      Defining the Actionsubject 12

      Defining the Outcome 12

   ELEMENTS OF A LOGLINE 13

      A subject 13

      A verb. 13

      An action 13

      An outcome. 13

   DIAGRAM OF A LOGLINE 15

CHAPTER TWO 17

THE KEYSTROKE KILLER 17

   WARNING RATING ALERT 19

   ABOUT THE KEYSTROKE KILLER 19

      COPYRIGHT INFORMATION 20

      FADE IN 21

      FADE TO BLACK 44

CHAPTER THREE 45

THE SUBJECT 45

   WHO ME? 45

ASK WHO?..47

   Logline 1 – Blaze as the Main Character..........................48

   Logline 2 – Matthew as the Main Character......................48

   Logline 3 – Judas (AKA the Keystroke Killer) as the Main Character..........48

BLAZE...49

MATTHEW..49

JUDAS AKA THE KEYSTROKE KILLER............................51

WILL THE REAL SUBJECT PLEASE STAND UP?...............51

   Subject Logline 1 – Blaze as the Main Character...............51

   Subject Logline 2 – Matthew as the Main Character.........52

   Subject Logline 3 – The Keystroke Killer as the Main Character..........52

CHAPTER FOUR...**53**

GET DOWN TO IT...53

THE ACTION VERB...**53**

WHAT IS -MY SUBJECT DOING?................................55

   Action Verb Logline 1...55

   Action Verb Logline 2...55

   Action Verb Logline 3...55

   Modified Action Verb Logline 1.................................56

   Modified Action Verb Logline 2.................................56

   Modified Action Verb Logline 3.................................56

   Modified Action Verb Logline 4.................................56

CHAPTER FIVE...**57**

THE ACTION DESCRIPTION.....................................**57**

IF I SAY JUMP...**57**

   Action Description Logline 1.....................................58

   Action Description Logline 2.....................................58

   Action Description Logline 3.....................................58

WHAT IS MY SUBJECT DOING AFTER THE ACTION VERB?............58

CHAPTER SIX...**59**

THE OUTCOME..**59**

ARE WE THERE YET?..60

   Outcome Logline 1...60

   Outcome Logline 2...60

Outcome Logline 3..60

Modified Outcome Logline 2...60

Modified Outcome Logline 3...61

Modified Logline 4...61

TWIST AND SHOUT 63

CHAPTER SEVEN..**65**

ENHANICNG LOGLINES...**65**

IT'S NOT PLASTIC SURGERY 65

RE-ARRANGE THE ORDER OF THE FOUR ELEMENTS 65

Re-arranged Logline 1...66

Re-arranged Logline 2...66

Re-arranged Logline 3...66

Modified Logline 1...67

Modified Logline 2...67

Modified Loglines 3...67

THE AGE FACTOR 67

Age Logline 67

Age Enhancement Logline 1 68

Age Enhancement Logline 2 68

Age Enhancement Logline 3 68

THE NAME GAME 69

Name Logline..69

Name Enhancement Logline 1 69

WHERE IN THE WORLD IS CARMEN ELECTRA? 69

Location Enhancement Logline 1...70

Location Enhancement Logline 2...70

IT'S MORE THAN A PROFESSION 71

Profession Enhancement Logline 1 71

Profession Enhancement Logline 2 72

THE MELTDOWN 72

Crisis Enhancement Logline 72

WHAT MAKES A PERSON TICK? 72

Character Trait Logline 1 73

Character Trait Logline 2 73

TO BE OR NOT TO BE CRAZY 75

Emotional State Logline...75

THE IMPACT OF DESIRE 75

Desire Enhancement Logline...75

MULTI-SENTENCE LOGLINES 76

Logline 1..74

Logline 2..74

Logline 3..75

Multi-Sentence Logline 1..76

Multi-Sentence Logline 2..77

Multi-Sentence Logline 3..77

Multi-Sentence Logline 4..78

CHOOSING THE BEST LOGLINE 78

Logline 1- For General Purposes..79

Logline 2 – In a Business Plan...79

Logline 3 - On a Website..79

Logline 4 – Use on a Post Card...79

Logline 5 – Use on a One Pager...80

Logline 6- Use on a DVD Jacket or Trailer.....................................81

Logline 7- Use on a Movie Poster..81

THE DO'S AND DON'TS OF WRITING LOGLINES 83

Do..83

Don't..84

YOUR TURN 84

THE SEQUEL 84

PRODUCING THE KEYSTROKE KILLER..85

THE KEYSTROKE KILLER FACEBOOK SITE 89

PHOTOGRAPHY CREDITS...**91**

INDEX **95**

ABOUT THE AUTHOR **96**

FOLLOW DR. MELISSA CAUDLE...97

BOOKS BY DR. MELISSA CAUDLE..**98**

THE REALITY SHOW RESOURCE..**100**

HOW TO SUBMIT **101**

NEW ERA IN SCREENWRITING **102**

HOW TO CONTACT DR. MEL **106**

OTHER SCREENWRITING BOOKS

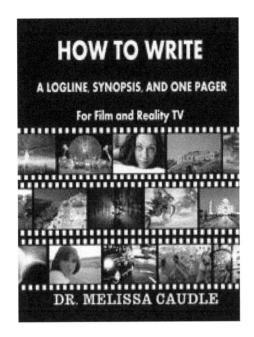

ALL BOOKS AVAILABLE ON AMAZON.COM, BARNES & NOBLE, AND BOOKS A MILLION

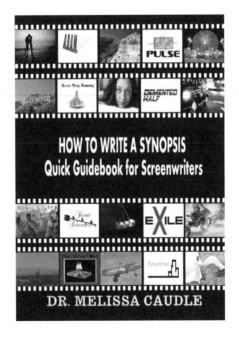

ACKNOWLEDGEMENT

Screenwriter Roger Corman, American film producer, director and actor, said,

> *"You can make a movie about anything as long as it has a hook to hang the advertising on."*

I say,

> *"Life is stranger than fiction and any movie or reality show should be about life and those who live it."*

I have to acknowledge the people in my life that have made it a wonderful life and interesting to live. There never seems to be a dull moment as a wife, mother, mother-in-law, grandmother, littlest sister, aunt, sister-in-law, niece, producer, reality show creator, director, screenwriter, actor, crewmember, colleague, author, mentor, and friend. If I were to write a logline for my life, it would be:

> After a severe illness, a former educator, turned producer and screenwriter, realizes the most important thing in life is to be with her family.

"Who needs a fantasy when I have my reality?" **Dr. Melissa Caudle**

SPECIAL THANKS

TO THOSE THAT HAVE ALWAYS BELIEVED IN ME, INSPIRED ME, AND HELPED MAKE MY DREAMS TO COME TRUE. YOU KNOW WHO YOU ARE.

TO JAMIE ALYSON, FEATURED THROUGHOUT THIS BOOK, AS BLAZE, IN THE SCREENPLAY *THE KEYSTROKE KILLER*, MAY ALL OF YOUR DREAMS COME TRUE. ONE DAY, I WANT THAT INVITATION TO THE ACADEMY AWARDS WHEN YOU RECEIVE BEST ACTRESS AND GOOD LUCK ON YOUR DEBUT ROLE IN THE UPCOMING *T.D. JAKES FILM WOMAN THOU ARE LOOSED: ON THE 7TH DAY*, DIRECTED BY NEEMA BARNETTE.

TO ALL OF THE PHOTOGRAPHERS THAT GENEROUSLY PROVIDED ME WITH THE PHOTOGRAPHS USED THROUGHOUT THIS BOOK. I ESPECIALLY WANT TO THANK SIMON HOWDEN AND SALVATORE VUONO FOR THEIR EXCEPTIONAL TALENT AND PHOTOGRAPHS.

TO MY FOCUS GROUPS IN NEW ORLEANS AND LOS ANGELES. YOUR FEEDBACK WAS ESSENTIAL TO MY WRITING OF THE BOOK SERIES. THANKS AGAIN.

TO MY COPY PROOF EDITOR, ROBBY COOK STROUD FOR YOUR DEDICATION AND HELP WITH THIS BOOK. YOUR EYES ARE BETTER THAN MINE.

TO MY FAMILY. YOU KNOW WHY.

DEDICATION

MY PARENTS
William W. and Helen V. Ray

MY HUSBAND
Michael Caudle

MY CHILDREN AND THEIR FAMILIES
Erin and Dimitris and sons Stamatis and Elias
Kelly and Roger Jr. and son Roger III
Jamie and Haunnard and to my future grandchildren

MY SIBLINGS
Denny, Livia, Caylen, and Robby

MY PEERS
Drew Brees, Neema Barnette, Nina Henderson-Moore, Gina Holland, Jamie Balthazar, Sharon Leal, Blair Underwood, Laurie Herbert, Dallas Montgomery, Jodie Jones, Jason Box, Andy Sparaco, David C. Kirtland, Tracey Davenport, Duane Gross, Michael Ragsdale, Jimmy Fallon, David Replogle, Salvatore Vuono, Dr. Carol Michaels, Nicolas Cage, Dustin Weeks, Roman Harper, Christopher Gray, Marin Lawrence, Cuba Gooding Jr., Mary Tyler Moore, Scott Moran, Phebe Hurst Middleton, Don Knotts, Sally Ann Robertson, Patrick Evans, Johnny Weir, Parker Armstrong, Nathaniel Baker, T.D. Jakes, Dr. James Meza, Shiri Appleby, Eyal Podell, Zach and Shantell Nasits, Ashton Phillips, Michael Douglas, Ellen DeGeneres, John Goodman, Malcom Petal, Mark Burnett, Tim Hightower, Tracey Miller, Martha Stewart, Donny Osmond, John Dupre, Madame Elisandrya De Sade, Govenor Bobby Jindal, Senator Gary Hart, Jonathan Rhys Meyers, Randy Quaid, Penny Marshall, Enya, Haley Reinhart, James Durban, Tom Cantwell, Diablo Cody, Brad Pitt, Nicholas Cage, John Landis, Tim Owens, Matt Damon and his mother Nancy Carlsson-Paige, Steven SeagalKevin Williamson, Piers Anthony, Dr. Felisa Wolfe- Simon, Beau Marks, Stephen Esteb, Robert Downey Jr., Shamar Moore, J.P. Prieto, Darren Sharper, Ron Lurie, James Woods, Kate Bosworth, James Marsden, Alexander Skarsgaurd, Drew Powell, Rhys Corio, Billy Lush, Dominic Purcell, Marc Friedman, Arlena Acree, Vince Vance, Brett Butler, Fran Drescher, Carmen Electra, Josh Gad, Anne Rice, The Swider Brothers, Ronald D. Moore, Sir Anthony Hopkins, Michael Heisman, Kevin Costner, Kenneth Johnson, Jamie Fox, Gordon Peck Jr., Kelly Marcel, Derrick Berry, Laz

Alonzo, Ernie Banks, Jeff Galpin, Ted Lange, Governor Buddy Roemer, Jaqueline Flemming, Suzie Labry, Bill Donavan, Lenni Kravitz, Rhys Coiro, Billy Lush, Anson Mount, Walton Goggins, Carmen Electra, Susy Labry, Michael Mann, Wayne Morgan, Steven Zaillian, Peter Frampton, Justin Beiber, Brittney Spears, Derrick Barry, Jimmy Kimbell, Ray Bradbury, Jim Morrison, Charlie Daniels, Janet Leahy, Glenn Gainor, Patrick Stewart, Geraldo Rivero, Phil Donahue, Senn Penn, Hisako Matsui, Emily Mortimer, Martin Lawrence, Nathan Scott, Joe Montegna, Stevie Nicks, John Lands, Jude Law, Stehpen Rue, Lance Nichols, The Olsen Twins, Blain Kern, Robyn Batherson, Lucy Lawless, Mike Anderson, John Andeson, Liz Coulon, Ryan Glorioso, Jim Morrison, Nancy Grace, George Flynn, Ray Fields, James Mance Jr., Sara Gruen, Ann Gibbs, Patrick Taylor, Sean Penn, Jonathan Frakes, Morena Baccarin, Kelly Preston, Connie Chung, Mel Gibson, Melissa Leo, Ken Follett, Criss Angel, Mathieu Kassovitz, Dominic Purcell, Stevie Nicks, Melissa Leo, Ally Sheedy, Gary Grubbs, Kendra Wilkinson, Anne Massey, Holly Madison, David Hebert, John Sayles, Bridget Marquardt, Graham Nelson, Beau Bridges, Melissa Peterman, Raymond Chandler, Elizebeth George, Lou Angeli, Jeffery Roberson (AKA Varla Jean Merman), Mark Cortale, Ryan Dufrene, Dusty Wilson,   Nick Phillips, Judd Nelson, Hugh Hefner, Michael Crawford, Radha Mitchell, Bill Klein, Jennifer Arnold, Benjamin Hurvitz, Eli Holzman, Amanda Stutevoss Coppola, Sheldon Lazarus, Jude Law, Jay Leno, Simon Cowell, Ellen DeGeneres, Paula Abdul, Morgan Freeman, L.L. Cool Jay, Queen Latiffa, Nina Garcia, Eminem, Pamela Anderson, Dorian Dardar, Adam Lambert, Andrew Gurland, Veronica Kelly, Kevin Costner, Adam Horowitz, Wendy Smith, Kelsy Grammer, Chris Koffer, Dean Develin, Michelle Nicolette Kowalski, Callie Moore, Wendie Malick, Lacey Chabert, Mark Haddon, Sylvester Stallone, Steve Purcell, Jim Jarmusch, Lou Angelie, Joe Hausterhaus, Janice Engel, Connie Chung, Former Governor Buddy Roemer, Suzanne Pleshett, Delta Burke, Rob Marshall, Isaac Bashevis Singer, Marie Scott, Thomas Moore, Lucy Lawless, Timohy Robbins, Jimmy Buffett, Jimmy Kimmel, James Franco, Simon Howden, Ken Follett, Jeff Davis, Jessica Simpson, Erica Messer, Ed Bernero, Jonathan Carroll, J.P. Perez, Simon Mirren, Foster Remington, Johnny Knoxville, Seann William Scott, Burt Reynolds, Willie Nelson, Lynda Carter, Tom Selleck, Ernie Banks, Eric Paulson, Sally Ann Roberts, Hoda Kotb, Vidal Sassoon, Debra Fisher, Andrew Wilder and Magan Laren, Wayne Morgan, Lance Moore, Reggie Bush, Evan Lysacek, Billy Ray Hobley, Tracey Portier, Chris Ivory, Jason Priestley, and Trevor Jones

MY BESTFRIENDS WHO ARE MY PETS
To my Chihuhuas Gizmo and Lola,
To my African Albino Dwraf Frogs Fric III and Frac

INTRODUCTION

THE MILLION-DOLLAR HOOK

"A short saying oft contains much wisdom." **Sophocles - Philosopher**

How to Write a Logline: Quick Reference Guide for Screenwriters takes the screenwriter on a journey through the maze of cutting down your 125-page script into one meaningful and powerful sentence. That isn't easy for most screenwriters. Just ask any one of them. They will say the same thing.

It is important for you to be able to gain knowledge and practice before the final crunch time of writing a logline. This book helps not only the first-time logline writer, but also the experienced writer who wants to hone their ability to capture the concept of a screenplay into one sentence for the million-dollar hook. One of three books in a series of quick reference guidebooks, *How to Write a Logline Quick Reference Guide for Screenwriters,* provides the screenwriter with a powerful resource for developing a logline.

The three books in this series are:

- *How to Write a Logline: Quick Guidebook for Screenwriters*

- *How to Write a Synopsis: Quick Guidebook for Screenwriters*
- *How to Create a One Pager: Quick Guidebook for Screenwriters*

Additionally, I have added to the series with my book *Inside the Writer's Mind: Developing a Script Using Your Past Experiences*. This book, like the other three in

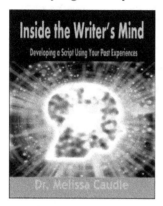

the series, uses the screenplay *The Keystroke Killer*. I take the reader on my journey developing the screenplay. You get to know a great deal about me as a person and the inspiration behind the screenplay. It is one of the most unusual books I've written. Many screenwriters find it inspirational. *How to Write a Logline: Quick Guidebook for Screenwriters* is important in many ways. First, it is compact and easy to understand. Second, you get practice reading numerous loglines for *The Keystroke Killer*. Lastly, it's the most comprehensive book on the market on writing and developing a logline.

ABOUT THIS BOOK

How to Write a Logline: Quick Guide for Screenwriters is the first book in a three-part book series. The other books are *How to Write a Synopsis: Quick Guide for Screenwriters*, and *How to Create a One Pager: Quick Guide for Screenwriters*. Together with this book, they precede my comprehensive book *How to Write Loglines, Synopsis, and One Pager for Film and Reality TV*. After several focus groups, in New Orleans and Los Angeles, the feedback I received from screenwriters and reality show creators was several of them didn't need to learn all three topics discussed in my comprehensive book. They thought it would be fantastic if I gave people the option of choosing the topic they needed to learn in a condensed format for ready access. In essence, they

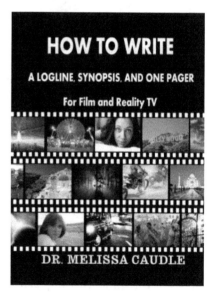

wanted a *Cliff Note* version on each of the three topics and the option to purchase individual topics.

They also loved the fact that the comprehensive book covered both screenwriting and reality show design, but felt that as screenwriters, they wanted screenwriting specific examples. I listened. This doesn't imply that a reality show creator can't use the quick reference guidebooks in the series. If fact, I encourage you to do so.

The knowledge and skill you'll acquire in these books certainly are valid and conducive for reality shows. My motto is, "You can never have too many reference books on honing your skill to write or sell your screenplay, film, or reality show." Eventually, I'll do the same format for reality show producers and creators as per their feedback. So be warned, that is in the pipeline.

Do You Need to Buy Both the Book Series and the Comprehensive Book?

Do screenwriters or reality show creators need to buy all three quick guidebooks in the series and the comprehensive book? The answer is as tall as it is long. There is a Native American saying,

> *"Tell me and I'll forget. Show me, and I may not remember. Involve me, and I'll understand.*

I feel confident that the three quick guidebooks for screenwriters are valuable and provide solid information. They are more of a show and tell in that you read about the subject matter and I tell you what they are and how to achieve the finished product you desire. You gain a solid foundation on each subject matter.

The comprehensive book, *How to Write a Logline, Synopsis, and One Pager for Film and Reality TV,* I consider the "involve me" book. This book contains a plethora of hands-on activities to apply the subject matter. This method allows for a true understanding for screenwriters and reality show producers and creators. I also strongly suggest you purchase *Inside the Writer's Mind: Developing a Script Using Your Past Experiences*. This screenwriting book is a must have for screenwriters to learn how to enhance screenplays and provide realistic expectations and characters.

Therefore, I'd say it is going to be an individual choice, dependent on how much information you need, as to whether you want to buy all three of *Quick Guidebooks for Screenwriters* and *How to Write a Logline, Synopsis, and One Pager for Film and Reality TV*. You may option for a combination of your choice according to your specific need.

The quick guidebook series is exactly as the name implies. Each book is a quick reference tool and applies more to screenwriters, as I do not include any samples for reality show creators. Use them in combination or as a "stand-alone" book. Whereas, the comprehensive book not only goes into detail for screenwriters, but also covers how to develop loglines, synopsis and a one pager for reality TV shows. This book contains examples for several screenplays and reality show projects unlike the quick reference guides.

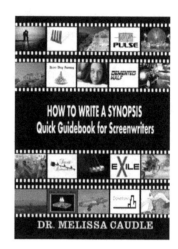

Please keep in mind that I do not repeat any examples from the screenplay *The Keystroke Killer* in the comprehensive book. Instead, I use several references to current films, reality shows, and those I wrote for my examples. This doesn't mean that a reality show creator shouldn't purchase any of the three guidebooks. In fact, I strongly recommend you do so. The information you learn certainly transfers to reality TV shows and the loglines, synopsis, and one pager you will need to create for your project.

In fact, I feel using all four books is similar to getting a degree – first you attend undergraduate school, then to become more of an expert in your field you attend graduate school to master your subject matter. Consider the first three guidebooks your undergraduate training level coursework and the comprehensive book as your graduate level and advanced information for true comprehension and application of learning.

It is my belief, as a former educator the more experience and knowledge you obtain about each subject matter will only benefit you. Knowledge is knowledge no matter how you obtain it.

It is important for me to address how I approach the quick guidebooks and the comprehensive book so that you can make more of an educated decision on which books to buy. Being able to differentiate between all of them may be the source of your answer in which books to purchase that benefits your style of learning and the topic you need to learn.

THE MARKETER IN ME

The marketing side of me thinks you should purchase all four books; e.g., the three guidebooks and the comprehensive book as well as any other of my books on production and creating reality shows. I have all of them listed in the Appendix. Each book is available at Amazon.com, Barnes & Noble, and other online retailers including my websites. The more knowledge you obtain the more proficient you become.

THE PRODUCER IN ME

The producer in me is reflective and suggests you purchase the individual guidebook book you need to accomplish the task-at-hand. For example, if you already have a synopsis and a logline, and you only need a one pager, then, by all means, you would only need to purchase the quick guidebook on creating a one pager. If you choose to purchase the comprehensive book, you still would benefit. You will be able to hone your logline and synopsis as well as obtain information that you don't get from the quick reference guide on creating a one pager.

THE EDUCATOR IN ME

The educator in me is decisive; and wants the best for you and thinks you need to start at the beginning with the guidebooks then purchase the comprehensive book so you get additional practical knowledge on all subjects. That way you work through your undergraduate coursework to the graduate level. The more you read and become familiar with a topic, you become proficient in the subject matter. That's a proven educational theory.

THE FINANCIAL PLANNER IN ME

The financial planner in me is money conscious and thinks if you can only afford to purchase one book, then purchase the comprehensive book *How to Write a Logline, Synopsis, and One Page for Film and Reality TV*. That way you have access to all of the subject matter. The only thing missing from this approach is you won't have the advantage of gaining the experience by applying the topics after reading *The Keystroke Killer*. I do find that learning by applying is beneficial. You may want to keep this in mind when making your decision.

WHAT ORDER TO PURCHASE THE FOUR BOOKS

No one can tell you that, not even me. You will have to make that decision based on your current need.

HOW TO USE THIS BOOK

To get the most out of this book please read the short screenplay *The Keystroke Killer* in chapter two at the appropriate time. **Do not** skip over reading it. It is essential to read *The Keystroke Killer* in order to get the most from the discussions that follow.

For those who prefer reading online or wish to download *The Keystroke Killer* onto their computers or IPAD etc., you may purchase the screenplay for a mere $1.50 by visiting any one of the following websites. This equals less than thirty-five cents (.35) per book. While you are on my website, I have a free newsletter you can subscribe to if you choose.

 Just look for the screenplay icon and click on it.

- www.onthelotproduction.com
- www.drmelcaudle.com
- www.therealityofrealitytv.com

You may also purchase a bound copy of *The Keystroke Killer: Collector's Edition* that includes never before seen pictures. This book is available from Amazon.com, Barnes & Noble, Books A Million, and my websites.

IN THE PIPELINE

I haven't written it yet, however, I have been requested by many people on my crew to write a book on how to breakdown a script. Okay, I will. Look for *Breaking Down a Script* in the Fall of 2012. It's in the pipeline and I have the go ahead from Open Door Publishing House. Thanks for asking.

CHAPTER ONE
LOGLINES: THE HOOK

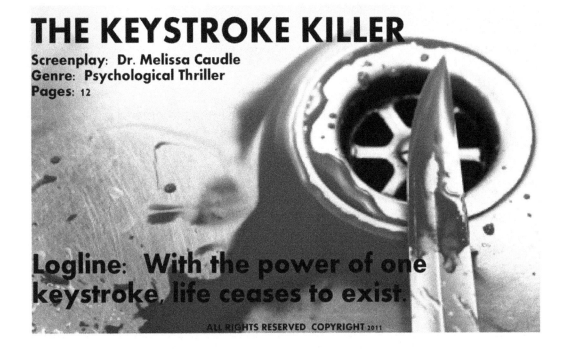

"There is great power in words, if you don't hitch too many of them together." **Josh Billings – American Humorist and Author (1818-1885)**

WHAT IS A LOGLINE?

When you pitch your screenplay, you must be able to hook your audience immediately. To do this, you need a hook, better known as a logline. A logline describes your reality show, screenplay, or film. It is a one-sentence summarization of that show's content. It's a short blurb, in the *TV Guide,* that ultimately clues you into the program. It is a calling card. That's the definition of a logline in the simplest form.

A logline accomplishes the same thing for any reality show, screenplay, or film. Designed to capture attention, it must be creative, succinct, and clear. Remember, you write your logline to grab attention and to summarize your project. So make it count and choose your words carefully. That way when asked, "What is your project about?" you don't have to manufacture something quickly off the top of your head making you look like an amateur. At all times be able to recite your logline. A well-written logline, when delivered with confidence, is emotionally intriguing and interest others into wanting to hear more about your screenplay or project.

Read the following loglines.

Logline 1

A woman has an affair and files for a divorce.

Logline 2

A young woman escapes the torment of her husband only to land in the arms of a lover.

Logline 3

After a violent attack by her husband, an abused young mother flees with her son landing in the arms of a stranger.

Logline 4

A murderer befriends an abused young woman with an infant.

Logline 5

Angela, an abused wife and mother, seeks revenge after a torrid affair with a serial killer who kidnaps her infant son.

The above loglines reference the same screenplay that I wrote in 2009 called *The Other Man*. In fact, I probably developed over 15 loglines for this screenplay in order to write the final logline to define the script. Why? The logline must reflect the screenplay and it takes numerous attempts to get it perfect. I have never gone with the first logline I wrote for any screenplay or project.

The Other Man is a complex screenplay, which requires a logline of equal weight. If weak, the script would appear to be as well. If too long and wordy, the script may appear non-structured. I felt like *Goldie Locks and the Three Bears* when creating the logline for this screenplay. I needed something that was "Just right" and captured the essence of it. This should explain how important a logline is to your screenplay or project. Often, producers weigh the "worthiness" of your screenplay by the logline. There must be a careful balance between the logline and the screenplay. One cannot overpower the other or fall into the shadows.

Of course, it is difficult for you to determine which of the five loglines accurately portrays *The Other Man* without reading it. That isn't my point I am making. The point is which of the five loglines grab your attention and increases my chance for you to either read it or want to see it? Which drew you in? Does one logline, over another, offer more information that you need or not enough? The difference between all five loglines is the enhancement factor. The enhancement factor provides more information and description with the use of adjectives and action verbs added to the key concept logline.

Can you spot the enhancements in the loglines? Examine them closer.

Defining the Subjects

I began each logline with my subject - the protagonist – a young woman. Notice in each of the five loglines listed below how I describe her.

Logline 1 – Defining the Protagonist

> **A woman** has an affair and files for a divorce.

In this logline, we know nothing about the woman. She could be old or young.

Logline 2 – Defining the Protagonist

> **A young woman** escapes the torment of her husband only to land in the arms of a lover.

In the second logline description, we know that she is young.

Logline 3 – Defining the Protagonist

> After a violent attack by her husband, **an abused young mother** flees with her son landing in the arms of a stranger.

By the third logline description, we obtain information that the young mother is a victim of abuse.

Logline 4 – Defining the Protagonist

> A murderer befriends **an abused young woman with an infant**.

As readers, we discover that our protagonist is not only a young mother with an infant, but she is also an abused young woman in logline 4.

Logline 5 – Defining the Protagonist

> **Angela, an abused wife and mother,** seeks revenge after a torrid affair with a serial killer who kidnaps her infant son.

The last logline description provides enough information for a reader to ascertain that our main character is not only an abused wife, but also has a child with the added fact that she is having an affair. This information gives the reader clues as to why she has an affair and why she flees. In other words, I added two adjectives to describe the woman; therefore, enhancing her description.

I do the same thing for the antagonist or the supporting character when I develop a logline. Notice as each logline strengthens as I define our antagonist.

Logline 1 – Defining the Antagonist

> A woman has an affair and files for a divorce.

At first, there is no description included in this logline. We only know she has an affair.

Logline 2 – Defining the Antagonist

> A young woman escapes the torment of her husband only to land in the arms of a **lover**.

The antagonist is a lover is this logline.

Logline 3 – Defining the Antagonist

> After a violent attack by her husband, an abused young mother flees with her son landing in the **arms of a stranger.**

I describe the antagonist as a stranger in logline 3.

Logline 4 – Defining the Antagonist

> A **murderer** befriends an abused young woman with an infant.

Murder describes the antagonist in logline 4

Logline 5 – Defining the Antagonist

> Angela, an abused wife and mother, seeks revenge after a torrid affair with a **serial killer** who kidnaps her infant son.

Finally, in logline 5, the antagonist is a serial killer. By adding the last adjective, "Serial Killer," We know that her lover is evil by using two words. The description of her lover as a serial killer provides conflict and we believe he will kill her. That's what serial killers do – they kill. Do you agree? Our antagonist moves from being a lover to a serial killer because of the words I chose to depict him. This transformation is a total change in complexity not only for his character, but also to the plot of the screenplay. The weight balances between the logline and the screenplay for *The Other Man*.

Defining the Action Verb

When describing the affair, it no longer is a simple love affair. We have intrigue, suspense, and romance. Does the serial killer lure her into the affair to kill her? The affair transforms from a simplistic version to the enhanced forbidden and illicit affair. Consider the following five loglines again and pay attention to the description of the woman's affair.

Logline 1 – Defining the Action Verb

> A woman has **an affair** and files for a divorce.

In the beginning, there is no indication why the woman has an affair. The first logline only implies she is filing for a divorce after an affair. We don't know what causes her to have an affair in the first place.

Logline 2 – Defining the Action Verb

> A young woman **escapes the torment of her husband** only to land in the arms of a lover.

We move to discover she escapes from the torment her husband because of abuse.

Logline 3 – Defining the Action Verb

> After a violent attack by her husband, an abused young mother **flees with her son** landing in the arms of a stranger.

Now our protagonist is a victim of a violent attack and flees taking her son with her. She wants as far away from her abusive husband as she can get. Because of the abuse from her husband, she takes action and flees with her son. "Flees," combined with "Her son," defines the action verb. We have an action description.

Logline 4 – Defining the Action Verb

A murderer **befriends** an abused young woman with an infant.

In this logline, the action verb is not defined.

Logline 5 – Defining the Action Verb

Angela, an abused wife and mother, **seeks revenge after a torrid affair** with a serial killer who kidnaps her infant son.

Finally, we discover that the love affair was torrid and the woman seeks revenge. We also see for the first time the name of the woman - Angela.

These enhancements appear after an action verb to describe what has happened once the antagonist is involved. After she discovers her lover is a serial killer she takes revenge upon him. It is a cause and effect relationship. One action propels the other.

Defining the Outcome

Lastly, each logline contains some sort of outcome resulting in the woman's action. Look at the loglines again honing in on the outcome.

Logline 1

A woman has an affair and **files for a divorce**.

The outcome of the affair is that she files for divorce.

Logline 2

A young woman escapes the torment of her husband only to **land in the arms of a lover.**

After escaping from her abusive husband, the outcome lands her in the arms of a lover.

Logline 3

After a violent attack by her husband, an abused young mother **flees with her son landing in the arms of a stranger.**

The woman is victim of spousal abuse and decides that she isn't going to take it anymore resulting in her leaving him. The outcome is she flees with her infant son and ends up in an affair with a stranger.

Logline 4

A murderer befriends an abused young woman with an infant.

This logline doesn't contain an outcome as a result of the murderer befriending our protagonist. By reading this, we can't tell where she goes, what happens to her, or whether she leaves her husband or not.

Logline 5

Angela, an abused wife and mother, **seeks revenge after a torrid affair with a serial killer** who kidnaps her infant son.

This logline is clear in the fact that the woman, Angela, is going to seek revenge against a serial killer who kidnapped her son. The outcome of "seeks revenge against the serial killer," provides deep insight into the screenplay and is forthcoming in distinct information.

THE FOUR ELEMENTS OF A LOGLINE

What I have just described in the five loglines for *The Other Man* are four essential elements and structure of a logline.

- A subject – indicates what or who is the focus of the screenplay.
- A verb – a single word used to convey movement.
- An action (action description) – the process of doing or acting. What is the subject doing?
- An outcome – something that follows the action, the effect, or the way something turned out as in a result.

Here are a couple of examples from well-known movies that exemplifies the structure of a logline. For each example, I provide a simple logline followed by an enhanced version.

Example 1 – Logline from *Gladiator* – Screenplay by David Franzoni

A Roman general seeks revenge against a corrupt prince.

Seeking revenge against an insane and corrupt prince who murdered his family and betrayed him, a Roman general becomes a gladiator.

Example 2 - Logline from *Minority Report* – Screenplay by Scott Frank and John Cohen

A cop arrested for a crime he has yet committed flees to prove his innocence.

A cop proves his innocence for a murder not yet committed in a world where criminals are arrested before the crime is committed.

Example 3 – Logline for *Wizard of Oz* – Screenplay by Noel Langley, Florence Ryerson, and Edgar Allan Woolf

A wizard helps a young girl go home after a tornado transports her to a magical land.

A young girl from Kansas transports to a surreal world and befriends three strangers on a journey to find a wizard with the power to send her home.

In each of the above examples, can you identify the four elements of a logline?

Let's break them down.

Example 1 – Logline from *Gladiator*

Seeking revenge against an insane and corrupt prince who murdered his family and betrayed him, a Roman general becomes a gladiator.

- Subject – A Roman General
- Verb – seeks revenge
- Action (action description)– revenge against an insane and corrupt prince
- Outcome – becomes a gladiator

Example 2 - Logline from *Minority Report*

A cop proves his innocence for a murder not yet committed in a world where criminal's arrests happen before the crime is committed.

- Subject – A cop
- Verb – arrested
- Action (action description) – arrested for a murder he did not commit

- Outcome – proves his innocence

Example 3 – Logline for *Wizard of Oz*

A young girl from Kansas transports to a surreal world and befriends three strangers on a journey to find a wizard with the power to send her home.

- Subject – A young girl
- Verb – befriends three strangers
- Action (action description)– on a journey to find a wizard with power
- Outcome – Wizard sends her home

All well-written loglines can be broken down into these four elements. These four elements are the basis for writing effective loglines.

To make it easier for you to write effective loglines, utilize the following diagram in a fill in a blank manner. The Diagram identifies the four elements: subject, verb, action, and outcome for the film *The Wizard of Oz.*

DIAGRAM – ELEMENTS OF A LOGLINE

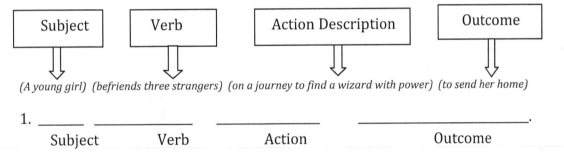

| Subject | Verb | Action Description | Outcome |

(A young girl) (befriends three strangers) (on a journey to find a wizard with power) (to send her home)

1. _____ _____ _____ _____.

    Subject   Verb   Action   Outcome

The Keystroke Killer

Screenwriter: Dr. Melissa Caudle
Genre: Psychological Thriller/Sci-Fi
Page Length: 24

LOGLINE
A world controlled by one person with the power to erase us and the fight to save us.

SYNOPSIS
Matthew, a tormented New York detective driven to catch the *Keystroke Killer*, a serial killer responsible for his sister's death won't stop until he finds him. When he meets Blaze, a young college student who resembles his sister, in Central Park, he races to save her when he realizes she is the next victim only to become responsible for her death.

TO OBTAIN THE RIGHTS TO THIS SCREENPLAY CONTACT DR. MELISSA CAUDLE
Drmelcaudle@gmail.com or 555-559-9632

CHAPTER TWO

THE KEYSTROKE KILLER

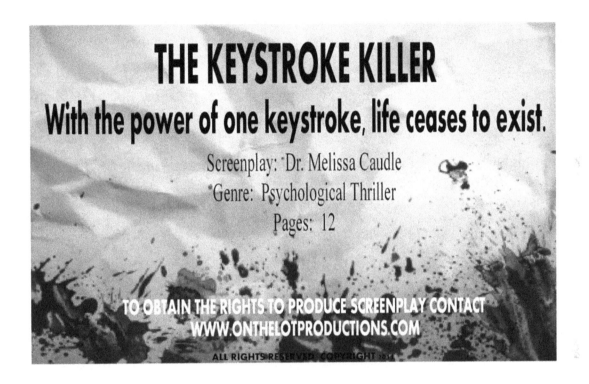

"There is creative reading as well as creative writing." **Ralph Waldo Emerson – American Author**

DON'T SKIP READING THIS

Now that you have a basic understanding of the four elements of a logline, it is now time to apply your knowledge and start constructing one. The most practical method to learn to write a logline is study how one develops for a screenplay. This is the method I use from here on out with the screenplay *The Keystroke Killer*. It is important that you read this screenplay as the discussions in the rest of this book center on the characters and plot. That way, everyone starts at the same point and learns to write a logline for the same screenplay. You'll have to trust me when I say, "There is a method to my madness."

For those of you who would rather read the screenplay online or on your IPAD, download it from my film and reality television production website at www.onthelotproductions.com for $1.50. This is an option for you, but it is not necessary for you to download, as it is included in this chapter.

Once you download *The Keystroke Killer*, you won't have to download it again for any of the other two guidebooks or for *Inside the Writer's Mind: Developing a Script Using Your Past Experiences.* However, if you would like to read the full script version for the pilot television show, Transcendence, you may opt to purchase a bound copy of that as well. *Transcendence* includes a special commentary by me, character breakdowns, beat sheet, logline, synopsis, and the treatment.

Additionally, there are many free downloads on my website including sample call sheets, prop lists, character breakdowns etc. for *The Keystroke Killer*. These in themselves are a great learning resource.

I hope you enjoy reading *The Keystroke Killer*.

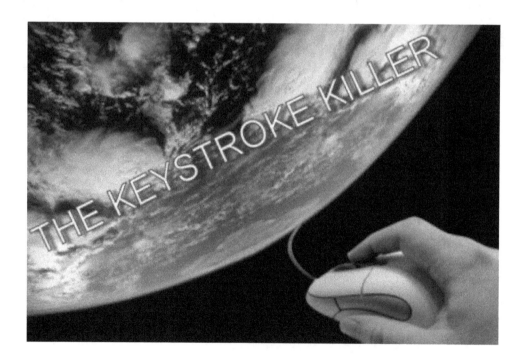

ABOUT THE KEYSTROKE KILLER

Genre: Psychological Thriller/Sci Fi
Pages: 24
Screenwriter: Dr. Melissa Caudle
Cover Model: Jamie Alyson – www.jamiealyson.com
Cover Knife and Blood Graphic: Simon Howden
Screenplay Cover: Open Door Publishing House - www.opendoorpublishinghouse.com
Copyright © 2011 by Dr. Melissa Caudle

The characters and storyline created by Dr. Melissa Caudle, in *The Keystroke Killer,* are fictitious and not based on any real people or circumstances. Any similarity to a living person in behavior, character traits, or name is coincidental. Likewise, the events in this screenplay never took place. This is a work of fiction. All Rights Reserved. Copyright © 2011 by Dr. Melissa Caudle. WGA Registered.

WARNING RATING ALERT

Please be advised that the screenplay *The Keystroke Killer* contains suggestion of violence and is not for the young-at-heart or for those easily offended by the idea of a serial killer. There are **no** profane words, nor does it include sex or nudity. If I were to rate it, I would have to say that it would come across as a PG-13.

NOT OFFICALLY RATED BY THE MPA

While you are thinking about it, join *The Keystroke Killer* Face Book fan page.

@

THE KEYSTROKE KILLER FAN SITE

**The Keystroke Killer
Screenplay by Dr. Melissa Caudle**

FADE IN:

1. INT. CAR - MORNING

   Normal road SOUNDS including New York CITY TRAFFIC.

   CLOSE ON A MAN'S EYES IN THE REVIEW MIRROR.

   As the car TRAVELS sunlight begins to spill revealing his face lost in deep thought. This is MATTHEW RAYMOND, 30ish, unshaven, dark circles beneath his eyes and disheveled. Age and stress has not been good to him.

   TRAFFIC SOUNDS soon fade to suburban quiet. The hustle and bustle of the city is gone.

2. EXT. PARK – CONTINIOUS

   Matthew's car comes to a complete stop at a playground filled with FAMILIES and a YOUNG COUPLE in love. It is what you would expect on a Saturday in the park.

   Nobody looks out of place except JUDAS, a transcendence creepy elderly man who stands in the shadows of a tree far from the activity. The forceful sun blocks the details of his face. He lights a cigarette. Smoke filters upwards polluting the sky.

   Matthew exits the car and closes the door. He starts to walk away and then returns to the car.

   He UNLOCKS the car with the remote, opens the back car door and retrieves a freshly cut garden-variety pink rose.

   He takes the rose in his hand, SLAMS the car door shut, and walks toward the pond in the middle of the park.

   Two SMALL CHILDREN lie in the grass and blow bubbles from a magic wand. They watch in amazement as the bubbles ascend high into the air and float away.

Matthew stops at the edge of the pond. He stands and stares as he holds the pink rose in his hand. Caught in the moment of tranquility the morning provides, his reflection ripples in the water as ducks swims past. He bows his head as if to pray. After a few moments, he makes the cross sign across his body ending the moment of prayer. He gently kisses the rose and then tosses into the pond, which adds to the ripples in the water.

He walks away.

BLAZE, early 20s, walks toward the pond with a loaf of bread. They pass each other. Their eyes meet.

A strange look comes across Matthew's face.

Both continue in their previous direction without speaking.

Matthew continues to walk toward a nearby park bench. He takes a seat and watches Blaze from afar. Suddenly, without hesitation, he bolts for his car and leaves.

Blaze is oblivious to Matthew as she focuses on the ducks in the pond.

Blaze opens the loaf of bread; and pinches off several pieces and tosses them in the direction of the ducks. The ducks quickly respond to the morning meal.

Blaze stops and freezes. A worried look controls her face.

A YOUNG MOTHER screams as she frantically begins to look around the playground for her child.

Blaze quickly turns and glances in the direction of Judas.

MOTHER
Tracy, where are you? Tracy!

Blaze turns her attention to the young mother.

3.

Judas extinguishes his cigarette on the ground beneath his left foot. He glares directly at Blaze.

Blaze runs towards the young mother who is now more frantic.

Just as Blaze nears the young mother, TRACY, a small child runs from the bathroom.

The young mother runs toward Tracy, grabs, and shakes her.

> MOTHER
> Don't ever do that again. Something
> bad could have happened.

Blaze stops and quickly glances over her shoulder toward Judas. He's gone.

Only the cigarette remains as small fumes of smoke rise.

3. INT. THE KEYSTROKE KILLER LAIR - DAY

Judas enters the lair and sits with his face to the wall, at his computer desk in the corner of the room. He watches Blaze on the computer monitor as she goes about her daily routines.

INSERT: BLAZE MONTAGE ON COMPUTER SCREEN

Blaze leaves the park. She changes clothes in her car.

CLICK

Blaze drinks a cup of coffee as she works on her computer at a Wi-Fi cafe along with MAG and JENNI.

CLICK

Blaze gets her nails done by a manicurist at a nail salon.

CLICK

Blaze leaves an upscale store.

END BLAZE MONTAGE ON COMPUTER SCREEN

4. INT. BULL PEN – DAY

Matthew sits at his desk searching through files. The sun glimmers through
the blinds. A DETECTIVE approaches and hands him a file. He immediately
starts to flip through it.

BEGIN MATTHEW MONTAGE

Searches his computer.

Eats a sandwich.

Drinks Coffee.

Rubs eyes in exhaustion.

Looks at the portrait of his sister on his desk.

The sun sets through the blinds.

Matthew packs up and leaves.

5. INT. LIVING ROOM - NIGHT

Blaze enters her small apartment. Exhaustion overtakes her body.

She places the mail in her hands on the coffee table.

Her two cats greet her.

She makes her way to the bar, grabs the cat food, and fills the cat's bowl.

5.

                          BLAZE
You two hungry? I know. I know.
I've been gone all day and left you
two to defend for yourselves. Just
turn me over to the S.P.C.A.

Blaze places the cat bowls on the floor. The cats begin to eat.

Blaze pours herself a glass of red wine and then sits on the couch.

6. INT. THE KEYSTROKE KILLER LAIR - NIGHT

Judas sits at the desk, face in the shadow, as he continues to view the monitor.

INSERT ON COMPUTER MONITOR: Blaze sits on couch as she sips a glass of red wine.

Judas lights his cigarette.

                                         MATCH CUT:

7. INT. LIVING ROOM - NIGHT

Blaze sips her red wine, puts down the glass, then opens and reads her mail.

A NOISE (O.S.) startles Blaze and she looks around. The same worried look as in the park earlier overtakes her face.

                          BLAZE
Any one out there? Meow Mix ... that
you? Tiger Lilly?

A KNOCK on the door. Blaze jumps.

Blaze cautiously approaches the door. She stops briefly to retrieve a large bladed knife from a vase that rests by the door.

Another KNOCK.

Blaze jumps again and looks through the peephole. There is no one.

> BLAZE
> Hello.

There is silence other than Blaze's own heartbeat.

Blaze double checks the dead bolt on the door.

> BLAZE
> I'm not interested. Go away.

Blaze puts her ear next to the door and listens. FOOTSTEPS.

Her CELL PHONE RINGS. Blaze quickly grabs it from the coffee table. She looks at the caller I.D.

> BLAZE
> It's you. The weirdest thing just
> happened. (click and static)
> Hello. Can you hear me?

8. INT. THE KEYSTROKE KILLER LAIR - NIGHT

Judas, face to the wall, holds his cell phone. The caller ID matches Blaze's phone. It's Mag.

In the background, the computer monitor shows Blaze as she paces in her living room with a cell phone in her hand.

INSERT ON MONITOR: Blaze puts the long bladed knife gently back in the vase.

CLICK

Matthew leaves the exterior of Blaze's apartment building.

9. EXT. PARK - DAY

Blaze jogs along the path.

Matthew sits on the park bench and watches Blaze approach. He looks like
he has been on drinking binge. His eyes are bloodshot. Yesterday's wrinkled
clothes and a morning shadow beard on his face does not appear to bother
him. The lack of sleep takes its toll on him.

He pulls a picture from his wallet and sadly smiles.

INSERT: Portrait of Matthew's Sister

Blaze jogs near Matthew. He returns the photo to his pocket. As Blaze
approaches, he stands and blocks her path.

                    MATTHEW
          It's dangerous to jog alone.

                    BLAZE
          Excuse me.

 Blaze continues to jog in place.

                    MATTHEW
          You're alone . . . a female. Haven't
          you heard? There's someone taking
          young girls from this park.

                    BLAZE
          That's an urban legend. I've grown
          up here all my life. Nothing ever happened.

                    MATTHEW
          That is until...

                         BLAZE
              Excuse me.

Blaze pushes past Matthew and continues her jog.

                         MATTHEW
              Wait! Hear me out!

                         BLAZE
              Freak.

Blaze looks over her shoulder.

The dark figure of Judas looms through the morning fog.

10. INT. WI-FI CAFE - DAY

Blaze sits at a corner table with MAG, her best friend. Both drink a cup of coffee and share the same laptop.

JENNI, the third Musketeer of the group of girls, hurries through the front door and joins them.

                         BLAZE
              About time. We'll never finish
              this project if we are all late.

                         JENNI
              Who said anything about being
              late. I simply forgot.

                         MAG
              How convenient.

11. INT. THE KEYSTROKE KILLER LAIR - DAY

Judas, face to the computer monitor's on the wall, sits and watches several computer screens at one time.

9.

INSERT COMPUTER MONITOR: Blaze, Jenni, and Mag.

He lights his cigarette that fills the air with smoke.

12. INT. WI-FI CAFE - DAY

A WAITRESS, who carries a fresh pot of coffee, refills the girls coffee mugs as
Jenni sets up her laptop computer.

> WAITRESS
> And you? Want some? Of course you
> do.

The waitress pours the coffee and walks away in a huff.

> BLAZE
> What was that about?

Jenni finally has her computer booted.

> MAG
> Not sure, but check this out.

> BLAZE
> What?

> MAG
> Another girl gone missing not too far from
> where you live.

> BLAZE
> Things like that only happen in movies.

> JENNI
> Third girl missing in three months. Same day,
> time, same amo.

                    MAG
I saw it too. The anniversary is tomorrow.
Alerts are everywhere. Check your text alerts.

                    BLAZE
You girls are freakin me out. Just
like a guy this morning.

                    MAG
What guy?

                    JENNI
Yea, what guy?

                    BLAZE
Nothing.

                    MAG
Then just tell us about this nothing of a guy.

                    BLAZE
He was watching me jog and then approached
out of nowhere telling me how dangerous it was to
jog alone.

                    MAG
Now that's freaky.

                    JENNI
We have to call the police.

                    MAG
The alerts did say to call the police.

                    BLAZE
It was nothing. Really. Now drop it.

Matthew enters the coffee shop.

11.

                         BLAZE
                    It's him.

                         JENNI
                    Him? Him who?

                         BLAZE
                    The guy!

                         MAG
                    You mean the serial killer!

                         BLAZE
                    Don't look. He'll know we're looking.

                         JENNI
                    Because we are.

13. INT. THE KEYSTROKE KILLER LAIR - DAY

     Judas, sits in the darkness, at the computer. The blinds shut.

     INSERT ON COMPUTER MONITOR: Blaze's empty apartment.

     CLICK.

     INSERT: A police bullpen with an empty desk.

     CLICK.

     INSERT: Blaze, Jenni, and Mag at the coffee shop as Matthew takes a seat.

                                             MATCH CUT:

14. INT. WI-FI CAFÉ - DAY

     Matthew sits at a table across the café and looks toward Blaze. The girls
     stare at one another.

                    JENNI
          He's following you!

                    BLAZE
          Keep your voice down.

                    MAG
          Why else would he be here?

                    BLAZE
          To buy a cup of coffee, like us.

                    MAG
          We have to call the police!

Mag reaches for her cell phone.

                    BLAZE
          Let's . . . just get out of here.

                    MAG
          You don't have to ask me twice.

                    BLAZE
          The coffee's on me.

Blaze retrieves a couple of dollars from her purse and places them on the table. The girls grab their things and head out fast. Blaze looks over her shoulder at Matthew.

15.   INT. THE KEYSTROKE KILLER LAIR - DAY

Judas, in the dark, sits at the computer screen. A black sheet covers the window.

INSERT COMPUTER MONITOR MONTAGE: Judas CLICKS to different images.

13.

CLICK: Blaze, Mag, and Jenni rush from the WI-FI cafe.

CLICK: Matthew sits at the table as the waitress approaches.

CLICK: Blaze gets in her car and PEELS out fast. She looks in her review mirror.

CLICK: Matthew leaves in a hurry from the WI-FI café and watches Blaze pull away.

16. INT. LIVING ROOM - NIGHT

Blaze barges through the front door. She looks around and deadbolts the door. She pulls the small table with the vase and knife on it in front of the door. She looks around then goes to the window and double checks the locks on it.

A strange NOISE (O.S.).

                              BLAZE
                   Meow Mix. Tiger Lilly.

A glass SHATTERS (O.S.). Blaze jumps. She runs and retrieves the knife from the vase. She turns toward the bedroom.

She stealthy approaches the bedroom just as Tiger Lilly and Meow Mix run out of the room in between her legs.

Blaze almost trips, but catches herself as she braces herself on the doorframe. The knife grazes the palm of her hand. It is not bad, but enough to be a nuisance.

A bloody smear remains on the doorframe.

She takes a deep sigh and covers her wound with the other hand as the knife drops to the floor.

She picks up the knife and heads for the bathroom.

14.

17. INT. BATHROOM – CONTINUOUS

Blaze pours hydrogen peroxide on her wound and applies first aid.

18. INT. THE LAIR – NIGHT

Judas sits at the computer screen with his face towards the wall.

19. INT. LIVING ROOM – NIGHT

A bottle of opened red wine sits on the coffee table. Blaze, with an empty wine glass in her hand enters from the kitchen.

Blaze pours a glass of red wine and flops down on the couch. She takes a sip.

She looks at her watch.

INSERT: Watch face set at 12:03.

Blaze stands and heads for the bedroom.

20. INT. BLAZE'S BEDROOM - NIGHT

Blaze throws all of her pillows from the bed. She pulls back the covers.

She walks over to her dresser, removes her pajamas, and then lays them out.

She heads for the bathroom.

21. INT. BATHROOM - NIGHT

Blaze begins the shower as steam begins to fill the room.

22. INT. THE KEYSTROKE KILLER LAIR - NIGHT

Judas sits at the monitor with his face toward the wall.

INSERT COMPUTER SCREEN MONTAGE:

15.

Blaze steps into shower.

CLICK

Matthew lies in his bed as he watches television. He picks up a picture of his sister from the bedside table.

CLICK

Jenni and Mag enter a movie theater.

CLICK

Blaze washes her hair.

CLICK

Fully dressed, Matthew exits quickly from his bedroom.

CUT TO:

23. INT. BLAZE'S BATHROOM - NIGHT

Blaze showers and rinses her hair from the shampoo. She dries herself and wraps the towel around her as water drips down her back from her freshly shampooed hair.

24. INT. BLAZE'S BEDROOM - NIGHT

Blaze puts on her pajamas and climbs into bed. She turns off the lights. She tosses and turns.

25. INT. THE KEYSTROKE KILLER LAIR - NIGHT

Judas, face toward the wall, watches the computer screen as Blaze tosses and turns in her bed.

26. EXT. BLAZE'S APARTMENT – NIGHT

Matthew stands in the shadows across from Blaze's apartment. He looks up at Blaze's window. He pulls out his wallet and looks at a picture of his sister.

27. EXT. PARK – SUNRISE

The sun begins to make peek through the branches of the trees.

Matthew sits alone on the park bench as he reflects on the wallet size picture of his sister.

A garden pink rose, freshly cut, lies across his lap.

28. INT. BEDROOM – MORNING

The sun comes through the beige sheer curtains.

Blaze sleeps soundly undisturbed by the morning traffic and the ambulance SIREN (O.S.) echoes from the street below.

Sunbeams hit blazes face.

Tiger Lilly and Meow Mix sleep curled at the foot of the bed.

Blaze awakes to the ALARM CLOCK. She fumbles to turn it off with her eyes closed.

Tiger Lilly and Meow mix, now awake, demand Blaze's attention as Meow Mix rubs against Blaze's face.

29. INT. THE LAIR – MORNING

Judas, stands by the computer and watches the monitor with his face toward the screen, as Matthew sits on the park bench.

From a distance, Blaze begins her morning jog.

17.

On another monitor, a young woman buys coffee at a coffee stand. He bends and presses the "Delete" key.

MATCH CUT:

30. EXT. PARK - DAY

Blaze jogs along the path.

Matthew sits on a park bench. He picks up the pink rose and smells it.

As Blaze jogs toward Matthew, he stands and hands her the rose.

> MATTHEW
> Please stop. I have something
> important to tell you.

Blaze throws the rose to the ground.

> BLAZE
> What, there is someone trying to
> kill me?

> MATTHEW
> I know someone is watching you. He is called THE
> KEYSTROKE KILLER.

> BLAZE
> I'm leaving.

Matthew picks up the rose.

> MATTHEW
> He killed my sister. She looked like you.

Blaze knocks the rose from Matthew's hand and pushes past him.

Blaze continues her jog.

>   BLAZE
> Freak!

>   MATTHEW
> Wait! The Keystroke Killer is after both of us. I'll
> show you.

Blaze stops in her tracks.

>   BLAZE
> What did you say?

>   MATTHEW
> I can show you the Keystroke Killer. He's everywhere.

>   BLAZE
> And, I'm going to believe you because... you're a
> freakin weirdo?

>   MATTHEW
> No, because it's the truth. You're next.

31. INT. THE KEYSTROKE KILLER LAIR - DAY

Judas sits at the monitor with his face in the shadows.

INSERT: Blaze and Matthew talk at the park.

                                        MATCH CUT:

32. EXT. PARK - DAY

Blaze and Matthew talk.

>   BLAZE
> You really believe this?

19.

                          MATTHEW
              He watches everybody, not just you.
              He's watching us now.

33. INT. THE KEYSTROKE KILLER LAIR - NIGHT

    Judas sits at the computer, face to the wall, and fixates on the screen's image
    of Matthew and Blaze.

34. INT. WI-FI COFFEE SHOP – DAY

    Jenni reads her book. Mag hands her a couple of dollars. Mag takes the final
    sip of coffee and walks to the door to leave.

35. INT. THE KEYSTROKE KILLER LAIR - DAY

    Judas sits at the monitor with his face to the wall.

    INSERT: COMPUTER MONITOR – Mag exits coffee shop alone.

    Judas places his finger on the DELETE keyboard button and holds it there.

    INSERT COMPUTER SCREEN: Mag dissolves into thin air. No trace of her.

    The screen goes black. STATIC NOISE.

    Judas gets his coat and leaves.

36. EXT. PARK - DAY

    Blaze and Matthew talk.

                          BLAZE
              And next, you're going to tell me
              he is going to kill me.

    Blaze's phone RINGS. It's Jen.

> MATTHEW
> None of this is real. You're not
> real, the world isn't real.

Blaze answers the phone.

> BLAZE
> What do you mean Mag vanished?

> MATTHEW
> You're next.

> BLAZE
> You're crazy. Now get out of my way.

Blaze pushes past him and runs away.

> MATTHEW
> (yelling)
> I'm telling you. Unless I can stop him, whoever this is
> or, whatever he is, will kill you next.

Blaze stops momentarily and looks Matthew eye-to-eye. She takes a deep
breath; then continues to run.

37. EXT. APARTMENT DOOR - DAY

Blaze runs to her apartment door with her keys in her hand. Her hand
trembles as she attempts to put the key into the hole of the deadbolt. After
several attempts, the key glides smoothly in.

She UNLOCKS the deadbolt.

38. INT. LIVING ROOM - DAY

Blaze quickly enters the apartment. She looks around as if someone watches
her. A worried look overcomes her brow. She locks the door. Double-checks

the door's lock, looks into the bedroom and kitchen, and checks the lock on the window. She follows the same routine as the day before.

Blaze paces the floor. She panics. She grabs the knife from the vase. She breathes rapidly in and out and hyperventilates.

She sits on the couch with her head between her legs as she tries to regain control of her emotions to no avail.

Blaze becomes faint.

39.   INT. THE KEYSTROKE KILLER LAIR - DAY

Matthew removes his revolver and uses the handle to BREAK through the window.

He climbs through the window.

He scans the room.

Above the desk is a wall with large computer monitors with multiple images of people Judas watches.

He bolts for the desk and searches through the drawers. He looks around the room then sits at the computer.

He moves the mouse and the computer screen on the desk lights up. Most prominent in view is Jen.

The monitor, left of Jen; which has been off, powers on.

INSERT COMPUTER SCREEN:

Blaze lays on her couch eyes wide-open. She is barely alive.

Her white top with blood splatter barely covers her breasts.

Blood oozes from several stab wounds. The long bladed knife with fresh blood lies in her lap.

She tries to focus on the room that is blurry.

>   BLAZE
>   (faint whisper)
>   Please forgive me.

40. INT. COMPUTER ROOM - DAY

Matthew sits with a blank stare as if he sees a ghost.

His left-hand rests on the keyboard and the right-hand controls the mouse.

INSERT: Matthew's right pointer finger as he presses THE DELETE key.

The screen with the image of Blaze goes blank. STATIC NOISE.

Matthew pulls his gun from his holster.

He SHOOTS the computer screen.

Matthew rushes out of the apartment. He is angry beyond belief.

41. INT. LIVING ROOM - DAY

Blaze's apartment is clean and untouched.

No evidence of her, blood, or foul play is in the apartment.

The door opens. Matthew and the LANDLORD enter.

>   MATTHEW
>   How long did you say this apartment was vacant?

>   LANDLORD
>   For a year.

Matthew begins to pick things up from the coffee table and expect them.

He pulls a chair over to a vent. He stands on the chair. He looks into the vent and then gets down. He continues to search the apartment. He searches for something specific to no avail.

He goes from one item to the next throughout the apartment.

He stands in front of the vase. A silver reflection shines inside the vase.

He looks into the vase and retrieves a knife. He pulls the knife quickly from the vase and puts it in his jacket unnoticed by the Landlord.

> MATTHEW
> What about the girl who lives here? She was just here.
> Her name is Blaze.

> LANDLORD
> You must be mistaken. The last person to rent this apartment was an old widow, Ms. Cavalier I believe. She died over a year ago. No one wants to live where a dead body was found.

Matthew's cell phone RINGS just as he finds a small hidden camera.

He puts the camera in his jacket pocket.

He answers the phone and continues to search.

> MATTHEW
> Detective Morrison. (beat). What do you mean Blaze Angela doesn't exist? I talked to her this morning.

42. INT. THE KEYSTROKE KILLER LAIR – DAY

Judas faces the wall. He sits at his desk as he talks on the phone.

                    JUDAS
     That's right detective. There is no such person.

43. EXT. PARK - SUNSET

     Matthew, distraught from the day's events, walks along the jogging path. He
     carries a long-stemmed pink rose.

     He places it on the park bench where he first sat and waited for Blaze.

     The sun sets over the park.

44. EXT. THE KEYSTROKE KILLER LAIR – NIGHT

     Matthew walks up to the outside of the Keystroke Killer's lair and stands
     guard. If looks could kill, Judas would be dead.

     Matthew pulls out his wallet and looks at the picture of his sister as Judas'
     shadow passes in front of the window.

                    MATTHEW
     This is far from over.

GUN SHOT.

                                        FADE TO BLACK

CHAPTER THREE

THE SUBJECT

"I always start with characters rather than with a plot, which many critics would say is very obvious from the lack of plot in my films – although I think they do have plots – but the plot is not of primary importance to me, the characters are." **Jim Jarmusch – American film Director, Screenwriter, Actor and Producer**

WHO ME?

I hope you enjoyed *The Keystroke Killer*. It was fun to write and return to something that I love – writing screenplays. Doing so gives me a sense of letting go and allows me to take my readers and me to a different place and time. It also allows me to invent people hopefully you can identify with in their relationships. Isn't that what all screenplays do? They tell some type of story about someone and some kind of relationship they have with others and the universe. You can take a blank white sheet of paper, or in my case, a blank white computer screen, and bring life to it with words.

The Keystroke Killer allowed me to escape from my daily life. I created a world controlled by one person with power to erase us, the fight to save us with Matthew, and allowed you to get close to Blaze, the next victim. Hmm...? That could be the start of a powerful logline or at least strong words for the trailer. That's how I always begin when I write a logline. I sit back and reflect on the screenplay and the character's interaction with each other.

THE BEGINNING OF A POWERFUL LOGLINE

All screenplays are about somebody or your protagonist. They define your screenplay's main character. The protagonist is the one character that you as the reader or the audience viewing a film develop empathy and draws you into wanting to know more about them. All events of the narrative plot revolve around him or her.

The antagonist is the principal opponent to the protagonist. This character is usually another leading role and creates obstacles that our protagonist must overcome.

There can be more than one antagonist and the protagonist can often be difficult to identify if they change roles throughout the screenplay.

ASK WHO?

In order to start writing a logline for any screenplay, ask, "Who is the screenplay about?"

 Let's apply the question, "Who is the screenplay about?" to *The Keystroke Killer.* If you skipped reading *The Keystroke Killer*, please go back and reread it. In order for you to gain a complete understanding of the concepts in the rest of the book, it is necessary you read this script. It won't take you too long because it is a short.

Now that you have read *The Keystroke Killer*, identifying the subject of the screenplay shouldn't cause any big surprise or difficulty. Just ask, "Who is this screenplay about?"

In *The Keystroke Killer*, there are three lead characters and several supporting ones.

The lead characters are:

- Blaze
- Matthew
- Judas AKA the Keystroke Killer

Our supporting characters include the mother, Mag, Jenni, and the Landlord.

We have to decide who is who in the screenplay to identify the subject for the logline. In other words, is *The Keystroke Killer* about Blaze, Matthew, or Judas? Not so easy is it? Depending on who you believe is the main character affects the way you write your logline. Consider the following.

If you think Blaze is the main character and you follow the four-element structure for loglines, e.g., subject, verb, action, and outcome, then your logline will start with Blaze as the subject matter. However, if you think it is one of the other two main characters, then the logline changes. For example, compare the three following loglines that reflect the difference for the development of the loglines as we substitute the names of the characters.

Logline 1 – Blaze as the Main Character

> **Blaze** rejects the notion of a serial killer and becomes his next victim.

Logline 2 – Matthew as the Main Character

> **Matthew** tries to save a young-woman from a serial killer.

Logline 3 – Judas (AKA *the Keystroke Killer*) as the Main Character

> The Keystroke Killer targets young girls.

In your opinion, which of the above loglines fit the screenplay, *The Keystroke Killer*? Unbelievably, during my focus groups, the discussion became very intense as to whom the screenplay was about. I wasn't surprised by this because I wrote the screenplay that way in order to allow for creativity and expression of the focus group to learn how to write a logline.

In addition, when you think you have more than one subject, which you often will in a screenplay, then that is a wake-up call for you that says to include at least two subjects in your logline. If I follow this advice, the loglines above transform. Look at the loglines now as I add more than one subject to them in the revisions.

Modified Logline 1 – Blaze as the Main Character

When **Matthew** tells **Blaze** of a **serial killer**, she rejects the notion and becomes his victim.

Modified Logline 2 – Matthew as the Main Character

Matthew tries to save **Blaze**, a young woman, from a **serial killer**.

Modified Logline 3 – The Keystone Killer as the Main Character

Matthew attempts to identify the Keystroke Killer that murders young girls after he realizes **Blaze** is his next target.

Have you come a conclusion with "Who" the main subject is for *The Keystroke Killer*? Let's discuss the pros and cons of "Who" the main character or subject is for the screenplay.

BLAZE

For those who think Blaze is the main character you probably can find supporting reasons as to why you think so. For example, Blaze is the catalyst that moves Matthew to reach out for her and she is the target of Judas as his "alleged next victim."

Every action in the screenplay moves around her. It starts with her in the park, she assists the young mother when her child goes missing, and we see Blaze studying and confiding in her friends, Mag and Jenni. We also see her apartment from her point of view (POV) as well as from the POV of Judas, the serial killer. Therefore, one could surmise that Blaze is our protagonist.

Then, to discount that Blaze is the main character and subject of our screenplay, she is only the pawn in the story to allow the plot to develop for the protagonist.

MATTHEW

To support Matthew as our main character, he is the person trying to uncover the serial killer, known as the Keystroke Killer. As a detective, from the detective bureau, he investigates Judas. He follows Blaze because he believes she is the next target. Throughout the screenplay, Matthew keeps a watchful eye over Blaze as she moves from the park, to the WI-FI cafe with her friends, and to her apartment. Matthew also meets with Blaze the next day and tries to warn her about the Keystroke Killer although he never calls him by that name. We as an audience know this because of the title, but it is never stated. Later, Matthew breaks into the serial killer's lair as he views on a computer monitor Blaze's bloody body. A knife lies in her lap. He presses the *"Delete"* button on the computer keyboard.

As the screenwriter, I don't reveal his motive. The reader is left to determine it. One thing I learned from Robert De Niro is never under estimate the intelligence of

the audience. They can and will figure things out without you telling them. Reasons for Matthew pressing the "Delete" key are debatable. Many believe he couldn't take looking at Blaze as she lies covered in blood. Others believe he is angry and tries to remove her from the Keystroke Killer's monitor so he won't be able to see Blaze again. In the end, Matthew goes to Blaze's apartment, after she is dead, only to discover from the Landlord she never existed. Therefore, I think as the screenwriter, he pressed the "Delete" key to get the image of Blaze out of his view. He couldn't stand looking at another victim at the hands of the serial killer who killed his sister. The images are too much alike and too much for him to handle.

Many other discussions prevail. Several people who participated in the focus group said that Matthew didn't know that pressing the *"Delete"* button would erase Blaze's existence from earth. Others insist his motive is to protect himself to keep from being identified as the Keystroke Killer. The audience never knows because it isn't stated in the short film screenplay. It is left to the audience or reader for interpretation. This aspect is developed in the pilot episode.

I do reveal in the end when Matthew shows up at Blaze's apartment he searches for the hidden camera. Then, when he receives a phone call from the Keystroke Killer who tells him there isn't any trace of Blaze and she never existed, as far as Matthew is concerned, he believes he is talking to his commanding officer. Again, that is unstated. However, he is speaking to Judas. It could be interpreted that Matthew is being set up

by Judas to take the rap for the murders of the Keystroke Killer. This plot twist and development occurs in the sequel and future episodes of the television series for *The Keystroke Killer*.

All of this gains support for Matthew as our main subject and not Blaze or Judas.

JUDAS AKA THE KEYSTROKE KILLER

I also can provide valid support that Judas is our main subject. After all, the name of the screenplay is the serial killer's name *The Keystroke Killer*. He is also the one that keeps appearing in the distance and the one who sits at the computer controlling who and what he sees on his monitor.

This raises the question as to how he is viewing everyone whenever he wants. Has he placed cameras everywhere and he can view whomever he wants with a click to the mouse controller? Moreover, it is Matthew who identifies the *UNSUB* (Unidentified Subject) and is being outsmarted by him. It becomes a cat and mouse game; but we don't know who is setting whom up. The only thing we know for sure is that Blaze is the conduit between Matthew and Judas, the Keystroke Killer.

Again, how you interpret "Who" the main subject is directs your logline development. That is why it is very important that all screenwriters know exactly who is their main character and who is the protagonist and the antagonist prior to writing the logline for any screenplay or film.

WILL THE REAL SUBJECT PLEASE STAND UP?

I have made a case for Blaze, Matthew, and the Keystroke Killer as our main subject. In reality, the characters and their relationships to each other drive the screenplay. I think you will find this true in most screenplays; therefore, the logline should reflect the characters and their relationship with each other. That is why loglines with multiple characters are stronger.

Look at the loglines again from *The Keystroke Killer*.

Subject Logline 1 – Blaze as the Main Character

> When **Matthew** tells **Blaze** of a **serial killer**, she rejects the notion and becomes his victim.

Subject Logline 2 – Matthew as the Main Character

Matthew tries to save **Blaze**, a young woman, from a **serial killer**.

Subject Logline 3 – The Keystroke Killer as the Main Character

Matthew attempts to identify the Keystroke Killer that murders young girls after he realizes **Blaze** is his next target.

In each of the above loglines, there are multiple subjects. We know the protagonist and the antagonist. Although these loglines are a stronger from the first ones presented, they still don't represent the tone or essence of *The Keystroke Killer* in my opinion. The reason is these loglines only identify the protagonist and antagonists (subjects) of the screenplay and do not target the true action and conflict of the plot driving Matthew, Blaze and the Keystroke Killer's interactions and relationships. I have more discussion on these topics in ensuing chapters.

For now, remember a well-written and developed logline for any screenplay is always a painstaking work in progress until the project is entirely finished and distributed. Likewise, the name of the screenplay changes up until the last moment. *The Keystroke Killer* has had numerous title changes during the development including the names: *Delete, The Watcher, With One Keystroke,* and *Cease.* None of them stuck. I didn't come up with the final name until after I wrote the treatment.

WHO IS OUR SUBJECT?

Blaze, Matthew or the Keystroke Killer?

CHAPTER FOUR

THE ACTION VERB

"Action speaks louder than words but not nearly as often." **Mark Twain – American Author**

GET DOWN TO IT

When you get right down to it, what is missing from each of the loglines presented in the last chapter is an action verb with impact. Action verbs indicate motion such as run, race, hang, ride, shoot, take-off, explode, marry, and wind which are reflected in the above action montage.

Look closely at the above action montage. Do you see the action each picture reveals? You get a sense of movement by looking at them. For instance, what movement do you see in the still photographs above?

Look at action verbs in "action." What is going on in each of the following pictures?

Picture 1

Picture 2

Picture 1 on the left, is a Boeing F-A-18C Hornet fighter jet taking off from an aircraft carrier. This multi-role fighter jet's design is for a "dogfight" to lead military ground attacks. It can carry a variety of bombs and missiles. You don't have to read the description of this fighter jet to know what it does. In fact, the image gives the impression of warfare.

Picture 2 portrays five horses racing on a racetrack. Even if you have never been to the races before you can visualize the action in and around the racetrack. You can "hear" hoofs pounding the track and the jockey's whips cracking as each horse barrels around the racetrack towards the finish line. Can you hear the roaring crowd?

Both pictures are different, yet; both evoke emotions. This is through the simplicity of each picture. The images clearly capture and define actions. The jet fighter is taking off from the carrier while the horses race around the track. I can easily describe both pictures by the use of action verbs "takes off" and "races" which captures the essence of each photograph respectively.

When you write a logline, the action verb you choose must be as clear as if you were showing a picture. Define the action with one word. In this case, a picture isn't worth a 1,000 words, you need one word to be worth 1000 images.

WHAT IS MY SUBJECT DOING?

In order to identify the action verb for your logline ask, "What is my subject doing?" Another question to ask is, "What journey is my subject taking?" According to whom you think the subject for a logline is influences your choice for an action verb. Let's look once more at the three loglines presented in the last chapter. This time concentrate on the action verb.

Action Verb Logline 1

When Matthew **tells** Blaze of a serial killer, she **rejects** the notion and becomes his victim.

Action Verb Logline 2

Matthew tries to **save** Blaze, a young woman, from a serial killer.

Action Verb Logline 3

Matthew attempts to **identify** the Keystroke Killer who kills young girls after he realizes Blaze is his next target.

Do these loglines have impactful action verbs? By changing the action verbs, will it modify the loglines? Most of the time it will and for the better.

Words of action, such as *informs*, *races, rescue,* and *expose* imply that something is happening. You can visualize more rather than infer from these words. Now look at the three revised loglines with the replacement of different action verbs.

Modified Action Verb Logline 1

When Matthew **informs** Blaze of a serial killer, she **discards** the notion and becomes his victim.

Modified Action Verb Logline 2

Matthew **races** and tries to **rescue** Blaze, a young woman, from a serial killer.

Modified Action Verb Logline 3

Matthew attempts to **expose** the Keystroke Killer who **strangles** young girls after he realizes Blaze is his next target.

Do you agree these loglines have more impact? Are they getting closer to what you think the plot and tone of *The Keystroke Killer* represents? With the exception of the use of the word "Strangles" in the third logline they are more intense. However, after reading the screenplay you know the Keystroke Killer doesn't strangle his victims. I used this word for demonstration purposes as it conjures a vivid image of motion. The word "Kills" implies murder but we don't know the method. I could write logline 3 this way:

Modified Action Verb Logline 4

Matthew attempts to **expose** the Keystroke Killer who **uses his power of transcendence to kill women and erase their identity from existence**.

After you get this far in developing a logline, a dictionary comes in handy to assist in the identification of creative action verbs. There is nothing wrong with using a Thesaurus to identify creative action verbs or using a handy list either. In Appendix A, of my comprehensive book, *How to Write Loglines, Synopsis, and One Pagers for Film and Reality TV,* I include a list of action verbs for your quick reference.

CHAPTER FIVE

THE ACTION DESCRIPTION

"Never mistake motion for action." **Ernest Hemingway – American Novelist**

IF I SAY JUMP

If I say jump, you can instantly visualize someone jumping. Maybe you visualized a child jumping rope or a horse jumping over a fence. The word "jump" alone tells us **nothing other than an action. However, when you couple an action verb with a** description of what is to happen or needs to happen, you have clarity. Now, if I say, "A horse jumped over a fence," or "The passenger jumped the line," you know exactly what I intend for you to visualize. That is the importance of placing an action description in your logline after the action verb.

You can identify the action description for your logline by asking, "What is my subject doing?" Identify where the action takes them after you wrote the initial action verb. In other words, it is part of the action, but it completes the action by describing it. Look at the three loglines from *The Keystroke Killer* this time focus on the action description and what each character, Matthew, Blaze, and the Keystroke Killer, do immediately after the action verb. The Action verbs are in bold print whereas the action description is in italics.

Action Description Logline 1

When Matthew **informs** *Blaze of a serial killer*, she **discards** *the notion* and becomes his victim.

Action Description Logline 2

Matthew **races** and tries to **rescue** *Blaze,* a young woman, from a serial killer.

Action Description Logline 3

Matthew attempts to **expose** *the Keystroke Killer who murders young girls* after he realizes Blaze is his next target.

WHAT IS MY SUBJECT DOING AFTER THE ACTION VERB?

To identify what the subject of the logline does after the action verb, ask the following questions:

- What is Matthew doing?
- What is Blaze doing?
- What is the Keystroke Killer doing?

The answer to the question of "What is my subject doing," immediately identifies who the real protagonist is as well as the action description for the main character. The action description of the logline immediately follows the action verb. It brings clarification as to what your subject is doing.

In the first example, by asking, "What is Matthew doing?," I determine that he is informing Blaze of a serial killer. In the second example, Matthew races to rescue Blaze from the serial killer and in the third example; he tries to expose the serial killer. After reading *The Keystroke Killer,* you should be able to answer what the protagonist does plot wise, in the screenplay. With this said, Matthew is our true protagonist and main character and the Keystroke Killer (AKA Judas) is our antagonist.

CHAPTER SIX

THE OUTCOME

"When I was kidnapped, my parents snapped into action. They rented out my room." **Woody Allen – Director and Actor**

ARE WE THERE YET?

As with any good screenplay, it is also necessary for a subject to have a goal or a major transformation. The transformation a character goes through in a screenplay is a character arc. The character obtains resolution to some sort of crisis or situation and as a result, becomes a different person. This resolution or metamorphosis of the character is how you identify your outcome for your logline. Ask, "What did my subject get out this?"

Also, ponder the question, "Did your subject undergo a transformation or did somebody else change as a result of what your subject did?"

Let's look at the three loglines again for *The Keystroke Killer.* This time focus on the outcome for each as indicated by the bold print.

Outcome Logline 1

When Matthew informs Blaze of a serial killer, she discards the notion and **becomes his victim**.

Outcome Logline 2

Matthew races and tries to rescue Blaze, a young woman, from the Keystroke Killer.

Outcome Logline 3

Matthew attempts to expose the Keystroke Killer who kills young girls after he realizes Blaze is his next target.

Notice that only the first example has an outcome highlighted in bold print. The second and third examples don't specify an outcome and we don't know what happens, nor do we know what transformation occurred to our main character Matthew. I leave the outcome for the last two loglines for *The Keystroke Killer* to your imagination.

Examples 2 and 3 are great examples of how not to write a powerful logline. There is something innately missing from them. Now you know why I asked the question in the last chapter, "Are the above loglines reflective of the screenplay *The Keystroke Killer*?" To me, none of them has so far because they don't state the outcome or transformation of our main subject. The closest one is in Example 1. This problem is one of most frequent mistakes screenwriters do when writing a logline – they don't include the outcome.

I firmly believe not to have any surprise element here; therefore, each of the previous loglines need further development in order to capture the true essence of the screenplay. When I include the outcome or transformation of the main character, the logline is target specific to the screenplay.

Listed below are examples 2 and 3 re-written to include an outcome for each logline.

Modified Outcome Logline 2

Matthew **races** and tries to rescue Blaze, a young woman, from the Keystroke Killer, **only to become responsible for her death**.

Modified Outcome Logline 3

> After Matthew realizes Blaze is the next target of a serial killer, known as *The Keystroke Killer*, **his attempt to expose him proves fatal**.

Can you tell how the loglines take a new direction and align more closely with the plot of *The Keystroke Killer*? Also, notice that I am beginning to use the name of the serial killer. Up to this point, I frequently refer only to a serial killer and do not always identify him as the Keystroke Killer.

Also for the first time, we are closer to having a logline that reflects the tone of the screenplay. We know that the screenplay involves Matthew, Blaze and a serial killer, now known as the Keystroke Killer. We also know that during the climax of *The Keystroke Killer,* it is Matthew's action or decision responsible for Blaze's death. He is the one that presses the *"Delete"* key, not the Keystroke Killer. Logline 3 reads, "*His attempt to expose him proves fatal."*

By Matthew having pressed the *"Delete"* key on the keyboard in scene 40, he killed Blaze in the same way the Keystroke Killer would have. How do we know this? Because in the screenplay, we read that the Keystroke Killer watches Blaze and Matthew go about their daily activities in scenes 13 and 15. Additionally, prior to Blaze's death, the Keystroke Killer "Deleted" Blaze's best-friend Mag as she left the WI-FI café in scene 35. If you didn't absorb these plot twists the first time, reread *The Keystroke Killer* looking for them in those scenes. Identifying plot twists throughout a screenplay assist in writing any logline.

Now for a different twist as a logline develops.

Logline 4 – Outcome Logline

> Matthew attempts to **expose** the Keystroke Killer who *uses his power of transcendence* to kill and erase all trace of their existence.

If I dissect the above logline, I can identify a new outcome of the Keystroke Killer's actions. This logline provides an exact outcome – all trace of the victims erased. Once the "Delete" key is pressed by the Keystroke Killer, everything about that individual is erased; e.g., the body, soul, and any evidence to support their existence. If you tried to find a birth certificate or their Facebook page, there wouldn't be anything to find. In fact, no one remembers anything about the person erased from existence. This leaves one question wide open to ponder – "How does Matthew remember his sister and Blaze when no one else can or does?" This plot twist isn't discovered until the sequel, or in this case, the second episode of *The Keystroke Killer* television series. (*The Keystroke Killer* is in development as a television series).

Logline 4 also aligns the screenplay in terms of genre. Although *The Keystroke Killer* is a psychological thriller, the genre transforms and the complexity takes on a new life with this logline. We move into science fiction. It remains a psychological thriller about a serial killer, named the Keystroke Killer, who murders his victims by pressing the "Delete" button on his computer keyboard. However, this gives way to the possibility that life, as we know it, ceases to exist because we all live inside of the Keystroke Killer's dimension – *Matrix* style.

The Keystroke Killer has a super power – *transcendence,* which are powers independent from the physical universe that we know and understand. There is a fourth dimension where the Keystroke Killer resides. In reality, the universe as scientists understand it has only three dimensions. The theory is we are limited to length, width, and heighth, and can only travel these paths. However, the spatial fourth dimension is a scientific hypothetical universe that attempts to explain the properties between our dimension and the fourth dimension in scientific terms. This is where apparitions (ghosts) reside. The fifth dimension relates to time and the ability to go from one period to another along a continuum timeline. This is the basic theory of time travel. As it stands at the present development, the Keystroke Killer can only travel from the fourth dimension to our realm during the present. Who knows, as the series develops the mastery of time travel may occur. It is something that I will keep in the back of my mind.

This brings us back to the development of the logline. The Keystroke Killer makes the decision on whether each person lives or dies and uses his power to transport people to the fourth dimension. In essence, they become ascension beings and pure energy. It's just a game to him and he gets to play God. We know for the first time,

because of his transcendence state of being and power to transport, he has to take the shape of a human (Judas) in order interact with our world's dimension. He has to crossover from the fourth dimension to ours and possesses a human form to interact. As with all super power villains, each has a weapon of choice. His weapon of choice; e.g., the computer delete button, connects his electric energy in his dimension to our realm. As the screenwriter, I can control this and make it up. That is why it is called fiction.

Every super villain has his or her Kryptonite. Matthew possesses the Kryptonite necessary to remember the Keystroke Killer's victims. The Keystroke Killer's super power isn't defined in the spec screenplay, but is developed in the continuing episodes as is Matthew's ability to remember those the Keystroke Killer erased.

However, the transformation to the logline and to the series could only occur once I reveal the Keystroke Killer's super power and the outcome of his power.

TWIST AND SHOUT

The Keystroke Killer has new meaning now as we gain a complete understanding of the antagonist and his super power. The plot also becomes clear as I reveal the back-story. This is certainly one advantage that readers of my books in this series have over others is being in the "knowledge" of the back-story. Others will have to wait as the television series begins. I felt that it was important to revel the twists and turns in order for you to grasp the full nature of *The Keystroke Killer* for the direction of the logline.

Jenni and Blaze - Actors Veronica Kelly and Jamie Alyson

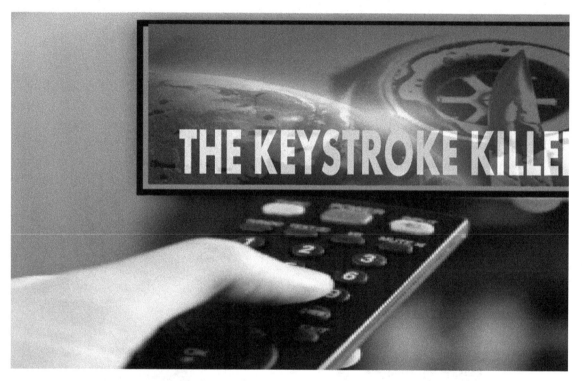

Be sure to join the Facebook fan page - *The Keystroke Killer Fan Site* to keep up with the film, new projects, and the upcoming television series.

CHAPTER SEVEN

ENHANCING LOGLINES

> *"Continuous effort, not strength or intelligence, is the key to unlocking our potential."* **Winston Churchill**

IT'S NOT PLASTIC SURGERY

The word "enhancement" means to make greater or make something better. In a way, we as a human society thrive on enhancement. From the beginning, man wasn't satisfied living in caves and freezing to death. Man discovered fire as a way to stay warm during cold freezing nights, designed shelter, and created weapons for protection and to make obtaining food easier. Soon, everything in life was better and improved.

We haven't changed from those early days. We still want everything improved. Just as I get an IPAD, the IPAD 2 came out. I can't keep the latest cell phone. There is always one better than the last. In addition, the last time I checked, music on CD's will be obsolete in a couple of years. Everything digitized is the wave of the future. We will move into a *Star Trek* universe. It's not just things and objects enhanced. As humans, we enhance ourselves. We lose weight. We gain weight. We exercise to build muscles. We apply make-up to our faces. We get plastic surgery. All of these are methods to enhance ourselves.

With so much effort in enhancing, don't forget about your loglines for your screenplays. You can enhance loglines with sophisticated style by application of enhancement techniques. There is a variety of enhancements for loglines available for use.

RE-ARRANGE THE ORDER OF THE FOUR ELEMENTS

To strengthen a logline, it doesn't matter what order you write each element. Often, by making an adjustment in the order each element occurs, a logline gains excitement and is more enticing to the reader.

For example, the loglines for *The Keystroke Killer* can easily be re-ordered and still maintain the clarity of the script.

Let's look at the three loglines we created so far for *The Keystroke Killer*.

Re-arranged Logline 1

> When Matthew informs Blaze of a serial killer, she discards the notion and becomes his victim.

Re-arranged Logline 2

> Matthew **races** and tries to rescue Blaze, a young woman, from a serial killer only to become responsible for her death.

Re-arranged Logline 3

> After Matthew realizes Blaze is the next target of a serial killer, known as the Keystroke Killer, his attempt to expose him proves fatal.

The above loglines are in the following order of necessary elements:

- A subject
- A verb
- An action (action description)
- An outcome

When I change the order of the four elements of each logline, the meaning doesn't change.

Consider the next examples and notice how the four elements are in a different order for each of the three loglines.

Modified Logline 1

Exposing the serial killer the Keystroke Killer, proves fatal for Blaze, after Mathew informs her of his existence.

This logline is in the following order: Action, subject, verb, and outcome.

Modified Logline 2

Matthew accidentally kills a target of a serial killer, when he tries to expose the Keystroke Killer.

This logline is in the following order: Subject, outcome, verb, action.

Modified Loglines 3

Discarding the notion of a serial killer, Blaze is killed by the young detective trying to save her.

This logline is in the following order: Action, subject, outcome, verb

Did you notice how the four elements are re-arranged, but all of them say the exact same thing?

THE AGE FACTOR

One way to enhance a logline is to provide clarification on age of one or more of your subjects.

The following logline for *The Keystroke Killer* informs the reader in one sentence the concept of the script.

Age Logline

Matthew races and tries to rescue a **young** woman, from a serial killer only to become responsible for her death.

Notice this logline doesn't include the young woman's name or her age. How young is young?

To remove any doubt of the age of the character, some screenwriters choose to include the age in the logline.

Age Enhancement Logline 1

Matthew races and tries to rescue a **twenty-year-old** woman, from a serial killer only to become responsible for her death.

By adding age to the logline, we get a better idea what stage of life a character is as well as the age range of an actor that could play the role. In maturity, a twenty-year-old is not as mature as a fifty-year-old woman is. A more mature woman is likely to handle difficult situations differently from a younger one. The age of Blaze in this logline influences the reactions of the character. Likewise, if we add Matthew's age it also changes the possible relationship between him and Blaze. If Matthew were sixty-five, he may be more of a father figure than a potential love interest. Look at the two following loglines to reinforce how the age of the character affects the logline.

Age Enhancement Logline 2

Exposing a serial Killer, known as the Keystroke Killer, proves fatal for Blaze, **age 17**, after Mathew, **age 73**, informs her of his existence.

Age Enhancement Logline 3

Matthew, **age 29**, races, and tries to rescue Blaze, **age 23**, from a serial killer only to become responsible for her death.

Did adding the age of our subjects change the way you feel about the loglines? For me it does. In the first example, I have to question the motif of a 73 year-old man with an underage girl. However, I don't question the motif of my under thirty leading man with a early 20 year-old woman. There could be a natural attraction between the two. Therefore, the age of your subjects has a direct impact on the visual image you present when included in a logline.

If age is going to be a factor in your screenplay, then I recommend you include it in the logline. Write your logline several ways, with and without the age of your characters and make the determination if by doing so enhances your logline or detracts from it. That is the only way to decide if it is necessary to include the age in your logline.

THE NAME GAME

Many times to enhance a logline, screenwriters include the name of a character. When referred to in a general fashion, the character lacks specificity and isn't personable. Look at the following logline.

Name Logline

> A detective attempts to expose a serial killer who kills young girls, after he realizes a young girl he saw in the park is the next victim.

The above logline reveals several things. We know there is a detective, a serial killer, and a target. That's it. We get all sorts of images in our mind. By adding names, the logline becomes more personal. Consider this version of a logline for *The Keystroke Killer*.

Name Enhancement Logline 1

> **Matthew**, a young detective, exposes the **Keystroke Killer**, when **Blaze**, a woman he met in the park, becomes the serial killer's next target.

WHERE IN THE WORLD IS CARMEN ELECTRA?

Adding the location can enhance a logline. Sometimes it is important to know where your screenplay takes place. By doing so, it not only creates a certain vibe; but also provides details where the characters live and provides an ambience for the surroundings. For instance, using *The Keystroke Killer*, as written, I can film it in any town or in any country. I can change the mood of *The Keystroke Killer* by placing it in a certain town or city.

Depending on whether the location is rural, suburban, or urban impacts the way characters interact. For example, people from a small community are more than likely to know each other. It wouldn't be a stretch for Matthew to know Blaze and want to warn her. However, let's suppose both are from New York City and he comes across her in Central Park. Her trust level with Matthew automatically changes. Strangers interact with each other differently from people that know each other.

Look at the following loglines and notice that by adding a location how they transform and provide a different mood and ambience for *The Keystroke Killer*.

Location Enhancement Logline 1

> Matthew, races in **the streets of New York,** to rescue a young women, from a serial killer only to become responsible for her death.

Location Enhancement Logline 2

> Matthew, age 29, races, and tries to rescue Blaze, age 23, from a serial killer in a **small Mississippi town**, only to become responsible for her death.

How does adding the streets of New York make you view the landscaping and style of the screenplay? Do you see the buildings, busy streets, and everyone rushing around?

What image do you get when you think of a serial killer in a small Mississippi town? Do you see a community of people? Local shops? Farmhouses? How would this affect the look of the film *The Keystroke Killer*?

Are serial killers different from each other if one is from New York and one from small town America? To know these answers is to understand the impact of locations when you include them into your logline.

Ultimately, it is the perception and vision of a screenplay by a director that dictates the style of the film and the locations chosen. The logline helps to guide all involved if a screenwriter includes the location and setting.

IT'S MORE THAN A PROFESSION

Sometimes the profession of the main character affects the storyline and logline; therefore, it is important for you to include it. In *The Keystroke Killer*, we know several things by the end of the screenplay. We know that Blaze is a student and that Matthew is a detective. We don't have any knowledge as to what, if any Judas does other that being a serial killer. He could be a computer programmer or for that matter, an omniscient being of some sort. We can enhance any of the loglines for *The Keystroke Killer*, by including Matthew and/or Blaze's profession. Look at the following loglines and focus on the bold print.

Profession Enhancement Logline 1

> Matthew, a **New York detective**, races to rescue a **college student**, from a **serial killer,** only to become responsible for her death.

Profession Enhancement Logline 2

> Matthew, a **small town detective** races and tries to rescue Blaze, **the local prostitute**, from **a serial killer,** only to become responsible for her death.

In these loglines, whom do you have more empathy for - the college student who just graduated from high school or the prostitute? You really don't have to answer that question, but it does change things up a bit. We shouldn't stereotype or type cast by making judgment on individuals because of their profession. However, whether it is subconscious or a conscious decision, the majority of people typically view a young college student to be more vulnerable than a prostitute who is streetwise. That is why it is important to consider if it is necessary to add a profession to a logline or not. The profession you choose for your characters can have a direct influence on how your audience views your characters and can have bearing on the interpretation of your logline by readers. Keep this in mind when you decide whether to put a profession of your subject in your logline.

THE MELTDOWN

One of the essential enhancement techniques for a logline is to include some crisis or turmoil that propels the plot of a screenplay. The crisis factor or a subject's meltdown is often a turning point and proves essential in your storyline. If this is the case, then it is also important to include it in your logline. Consider the following logline from *The Keystroke Killer.*

Crisis Enhancement Logline

> **Haunted by his sister's death**, Matthew, a young New York detective, races to rescue Blaze, from a serial killer, only to become responsible for her death.

By enhancing the logline for *The Keystroke Killer* with a crisis that involves Matthew, we get a clear understanding as to why our young detective is adamant in saving Blaze. After reading this logline, it makes you wonder if his sister was also a victim of the serial killer. The only clue throughout the screenplay for *The Keystroke Killer* is in scene 30 when Matthew tells Blaze that his sister was already a victim and she looks just like her. It provides motif to our detective as well as enhances the logline.

WHAT MAKES A PERSON TICK?

To enhance a logline further, use adjectives to describe a subject's character trait. Character traits come in all forms and behaviors to make a subject more interesting and diverse. Sample character traits include emotions, whereas others describe behaviors. The goal of adding an adjective that describes the character trait for the subject is to tell us something about him or her.

Is the character fearless? Dishonest? Selfish? Ambitious? Each trait directs how the character acts. There are numerous character traits to choose. See how the following loglines change in tone and direction for *The Keystroke Killer* after I enhance them to include character traits for Blaze and Matthew.

Character Trait Logline 1

> Matthew, a **fearless** New York detective, races to rescue Blaze, a **tormented schizophrenic,** from a serial killer only to become responsible for her death.

Alter Ego, Raven, from the film *Demented Half* - written by Dr. Mel Caudle. Featured actor is Jamie Alyson.

Character Trait Logline 2

> Haunted by his sister's death, Matthew, a **tormented** New York detective, races to rescue Blaze, a beautiful college student, **who resembles his sibling**, from a serial killer only to become responsible for her death.

Alter Ego, Angel, from the film *Demented Half* - written by Dr. Mel Caudle. Featured actor is Jamie Alyson.

By enhancing your logline with a character trait, it also adds a dramatic effect and makes it more interesting and intriguing.

We learn a great deal about Matthew once a character trait was added to the first logline. We now know Matthew is fearless and not scared of anyone, especially the Keystroke Killer. We also learn in Logline 1 that Blaze has a psychiatric problem – she suffers from schizophrenia. In logline 2, we learn Blaze looks like Matthews sister. His sister's death haunts him. Because of his sister's death, our fearless detective is now a tormented one.

In both examples, the complexity of the logline changes by adding the character traits for the subjects. In the end, these adjectives dictate how a director will view the character and how an actor portrays them. That is how important adding a character trait is and the potential affect they have on a logline. Use them wisely.

TO BE OR NOT TO BE CRAZY

Often, if you include the emotional state a character is in, it provides an element of enhancement. All great screenplays the main subject goes through some sort of an emotional journey. Only include the emotional journey in your logline if by doing so enhances it. Otherwise, the enhancement will clutter the logline. Instead of gaining the attention a screenwriter desires for the logline, over use of enhancements tend to drive a reader away. Now look at the enhanced logline for *The Keystroke Killer*.

Emotional State Logline

> Matthew, a young **grieving** detective, exposes the Keystroke Killer, when Blaze, a woman he met in the park, becomes the serial killer's next target.

The enhancement of the emotional state of Matthew takes us on a complete journey in this logline. We know he is grieving. As a human race, we all are able to identify with this emotion as for most human emotions. Therefore, when you include an emotion into your logline, make sure it is clear and that the emotion is valid for the character. For *The Keystroke Killer*, we know Matthew lost his sister when he provides that information to Blaze in the park. We can only assume that he is grieving. However, it is a valid assumption that we can make. There is one line in the screenplay that provides the reason Matthew is after the serial killer – Blaze looks like his sister who the Keystroke Killer murdered.

THE IMPACT OF DESIRE

You can also zero in on a basic desire your subject wants in order to enhance a logline. Adding a desire almost always grabs the attention of the reader. It also adds flair and spice. The impact for the logline for *The Keystroke Killer* again changes to reveal something about our main character when we add a desire.

Desire Enhancement Logline

> Haunted by his sister's death, Matthew, a tormented New York detective, **driven to catch the serial killer responsible for his sister's death**, races to rescue Blaze, only to become responsible for her death.

For the first time in several loglines, we understand what drives Matthew. It isn't that he wants to save Blaze; it is Blaze provides the avenue to catch the serial killer who killed his sister. That's a huge switch in direction for the logline. This direction is achieved after a desire propelling Matthew is added to the logline.

MULTI-SENTENCE LOGLINES

Another way to bring a dramatic flair to your logline is to use a multi-sentence logline with several of the enhancing features. For example, let's examine several multi-sentence loglines for *The Keystroke Killer*.

Multi-Sentence Logline 1

> Matthew, a fearless New York detective, races to catch the Keystroke Killer, a serial killer who targets young women. After Blaze, a tormented schizophrenic, becomes the next target, Matthew races to stop him but involves himself in her death.

Multi-Sentence Logline 2

Haunted by his sister's death, Matthew, a tormented New York detective, is determined to catch her killer. When Blaze, a beautiful college student who resembles his sibling, becomes the next target, he races to save only to become responsible for her death.

Multi-Sentence Example 3

Matthew, races in the streets of New York to rescue Blaze, a young women who resembles his sister from a serial killer. When he informs Blaze that she is his target, he is set-up and is responsible for her death.

Multi-Sentence Example 4

Haunted by his sister's death, Matthew, a tormented New York detective is driven to catch the Keystroke Killer, a serial killer responsible for his sister's death. When he meets Blaze, young college student who resembles his sister, in Central Park, he races to save her when he realizes she is the next victim only to become responsible for her death.

CHOOSING THE BEST LOGLINE

Now you are familiar with a plethora of loglines for *The Keystroke Killer.* You have read them in simple versions as well as enhanced.

Do you have a favorite one or style? If so, you could be developing a pattern in which you like for loglines to read. This tells me a lot about the types of loglines you will create.

You may like loglines that start with the action words or those that begin with the subject. Three sentence or two sentence loglines might read better to you. In the end, you will develop your own style and pattern. Nevertheless, how do you know which one is the right one? Now that is the million-dollar contract question.

There isn't really a right or wrong logline as long as it is well-written and includes all of the elements. For me, it is always been the one that captures the essence of the screenplay. I also choose a logline according to how I am going to use it. To offer clarification, if I am presenting a business plan, I may choose a short one-sentence logline on my cover and then follow-up on the inside of the plan with an enhanced version, followed by the two or three-sentence logline on the one pager. The one pager is the one sheet that describes your project. I also use a completely different version on the DVD jacket or EPK press packet.

Let's look at several loglines I created throughout this book and how and why I would use each.

Logline 1- For General Purposes

> Matthew, races in the streets of New York to rescue a young women, from a serial killer only to become responsible for her death.

This logline is short and straight to the point. I don't really need to enhance it to use it for general purposes when I introduce the project. It is self-explanatory and offers just enough information about *The Keystroke Killer* without going into a great deal. It is also easy to memorize.

Logline 2 – In a Business Plan

> Haunted by his sister's death, Matthew, a grieving New York detective, driven to catch the serial killer responsible for his sister's death, races to rescue Blaze, only to become responsible for her death.

When presenting a business plan you will want to provide more detail about your screenplay, especially including what drives your characters. For *The Keystroke Killer*, it is important for anyone going to read the business plan to know upfront what motivates Matthew; and why he feels like he does toward Blaze. This above logline provides that.

Logline 3 - On a Website

> Haunted by his sister's death, Matthew, a tormented New York detective, driven to catch the serial killer responsible for his sister's death, races to rescue Blaze, only to become responsible for her death.

People who surf the web usually look for something different from what an investor seeks. If they desire to learn more about the project they want to know who is involved, the plot, and where it takes place. The above logline for *The Keystroke Killer* captures those three critical areas.

Logline 4 – Use on a Post Card

> A world controlled by one person with power to erase us, and the fight to save us.

Sometimes to gain attention you might mail a post card with a logline. When I do, I like to use a logline consistent with what you would read listed in the TV Guide. Often, this type of logline never includes the subject's names, is succinct, and short.

Logline 5 – Use on a One Pager

> Haunted by his sister's death, Matthew, a tormented New York detective driven to catch the Keystroke Killer, a serial killer responsible for his sister's death, won't stop until he finds him. When he meets Blaze, a young college student who resembles his sister, in Central Park, he races to save her when he realizes she is the next victim only to become responsible for her death.

By definition, the reason for a one pager is to provide as much information about your screenplay as you can on a single page. The above logline captures the three acts of the screenplay *The Keystroke Killer*. Again, if you need more information on how to create a one pager, refer to my other books – *How to Create a One Pager: Quick Guidebook for Screenwriters* or *How to Write Loglines, Synopsis, and One Pager for Screenwriters and Reality TV*.

Logline 6- Use on a DVD Jacket or Trailer

With the power of one keystroke, life of a young woman ceases.

This is the first time I have really discussed this logline, although I have featured it in the graphics in the first and last chapters of this book. This logline is unique from all of the others. I call it a "Teaser Logline." The reason it is a teaser logline is that it teases a potential viewer by not giving away too much information, but just enough to let them know that a young woman dies. This logline attracts your attention and increases your curiosity about the project. This is perfect for a DVD Jacket or placement inside a trailer. I could also include it on the front page of an EPK package.

Logline 7 – Use on a Movie Poster

Matthew attempts to expose the Keystroke Killer who uses his power of transcendence to kill and erase all trace of their existence.

Movie posters are one necessity you must have after your screenplay is a film. Posters attract people toward your movie. Often, collectors of movie memorabilia and fans seek posters. Posters become especially important at your screening for marquee placement in movie theaters. At times, production companies place their logline or at a minimum a tagline on posters. The more familiar you are with the types and style of movie posters the better you will become at knowing what you want for yours. Graphic artists refer to your logline to create a poster.

Matthew attempts to expose the Keystroke Killer who uses his power of transcendence to kill and erase all trace of their existence.

ON THE LOT PRODUCTIONS,LLC introduces
JAMIE ALYSON
in Dr. Melissa Caudle's
"THE KEYSTROKE KILLER"

Starring

FREDERICK PALE as Matthew

*JAMIE ALYSON as Blaze *THOMAS PAIN as Judas *VERONICA KELLY as Mag *KELLY MOLINA as Jenni *MICHAEL FREEBOLT as the Landlord *Music by HELEN RAY and DR. MEL CAUDLE *Director of Photography by Roger Molina Jr . *Producer/Director/Screenwriter DR. MELISSA CAUDLE

Distributed by On the Lot Productions, LLC.

NOW SHOWING THRU JAN 2012   **PG-13**

FINAL LOGLINE DEVELOPMENT

By now, you have a thorough foundation on logline development including a plethora of enhancement techniques. You may have thought I forgot the following logline. For the last time, look at this logline below.

> Matthew attempts to expose the Keystroke Killer who uses his power of transcendence to kill women and erase their identity from existence.

I deliberately did not use the above logline in my enhancement examples in this book because I want you to practice developing a logline using this one as your starting point.   Manipulate the logline following the guidelines I presented throughout this book by rearranging the subject, verb, action description, and outcome. Then apply the enhancement techniques you learned. Be sure to think of the back-story for the Keystroke Killer's character – a transcendent entity with a super power when brainstorming your loglines. Write 15 to 20 loglines until you come up with the one you like the best. Practice will help you to write your own loglines for any screenplay or film.

YOUR TURN

I'd love to see the final logline you write. If I decide to use your logline on my website(s), I will give you full credit for writing the logline. Who knows, it could be included in one of my books or articles with your name printed as the author of that example. Send your logline to drmelcaudle@gmail.com. In the subject line, put "KSK Logline Submission."

THE DO'S AND DON'TS OF WRITING LOGLINES

First, please keep in mind that it is not necessary to use all of the enhancement techniques when developing a logline. Please don't overdo it. With that in mind, here are the Do's and Don'ts of writing a logline. I have listed them for you in a compact summary.

Do

> ➢ Take time to develop your logline, but develop it first before your concept.
> ➢ Hone and polish your logline throughout the writing phase.
> ➢ Up to the last moment, consider your logline as a work in progress.
> ➢ Use enhancement techniques to develop your logline.

➢ Write at least 12 different loglines for your screenplay, film, or reality show. Manipulate them in different order using different verbs and enhancements. One of them you will fall in love with.

➢ Make sure that your logline sounds fantastic.

➢ Your logline should be easy to remember and recite instantly when requested.

➢ Ask your friends and relatives which logline you created sticks with them.

➢ Be open to suggestions from others.

➢ Keep your logline to one sentence unless you need a multi-sentence logline for your business plan or one pager.

➢ Practice writing loglines by reversing the order of the four elements. They don't always have to appear in the same order.

➢ For added spice to your logline, feel free to add what type of genre your screenplay falls.

➢ Focus on the uniqueness of your project.

➢ Be brief.

➢ Capture the essence of the screenplay.

➢ Know the purpose of your logline and where you will be using it.

Don't

➢ Don't include the entire concept by telling the entire plot.

➢ Don't list every character in the screenplay.

➢ Never use analogies such as, "It's the Muppets meeting Indiana Jones." It's the mark of an amateur.

➢ Never use clichés.

➢ Never say your screenplay is absolutely the best on the market unless you created an Academy award winning film and the Oscar is on your fireplace mantle.

➢ Don't complicate your logline by using words nobody understands but you. Keep them simple, but use enticing words. That's the *epistemological* assumption of loglines.

➢ Never go over more than three sentences.

THE SEQUEL TO KSK

I am interested in reading what you as a screenwriter can do in terms of writing a spec sequel script for *The Keystroke Killer*. Remember that I am turning this into a television series; therefore, I need 62 episodes to complete a five-year deal, no longer than 45 pages each. *The Keystroke Killer* and the characters created are copyright protected and trademarked by me. However, I encourage your spec script submissions based off my screenplay as long as you put characters created by Dr. Melissa Caudle. The parameters for the spec script are:

- No longer than 45 pages.

- Each spec script must have its own title to reflect your episode. Every title should begin with "KSK" followed by something catchy that encompasses the plot of the episode. FORMAT: *KSK: _____.*

    Example Titles
    KSK: Pandora's Box
    KSK: Bad Luck Blues
    KSK: Beneath Still Waters

- Include a cover sheet with the title, episode name, screenwriter's name, contact information; characters created by Dr. Melissa Caudle, and WGA registration number. (Refer to the below format).

THE KEYSTROKE KILLER

Episode Title: _____

WRITTEN BY
YOUR NAME

Characters created by Dr. Melissa Caudle
Based from the original screenplay
The Keystroke Killer 2011

Your Name
Address

Email:
Phone:

WGA #: _____

Sample Cover Sheet for KSK Submission

- Correctly format the spec script; e.g., scene number, slug line, action description, dialogue (Final Draft or Celtx is the best to use to format)

Sample Scene Format

44. EXT. THE KEYSTROKE KILLER LAIR – NIGHT

Matthew walks up to the outside of the Keystroke Killer's lair and stands guard. If looks could kill, Judas would be dead.

Matthew pulls out his wallet and looks at the picture of his sister as Judas passes in front of the window.

                                  MATTHEW
                    This is far from over.

GUN SHOT.

- You must register your script with the WGA or U.S. Library of Congress. Both my production company and publisher, nor I can accept responsibility for unregistered scripts, we will not read them and we will throw them away.

- Must include Matthew searching for the Keystroke Killer's identity. Although he discovered the lair, Judas has now vacated it and moved to another secret location. Matthew continues to search for him throughout the series to avenge his sister's death as well as Blaze's.

- You can use flashbacks from the original screenplay.

- CANNOT reveal the Keystroke Killer's face or identity. He must always be in the shadows, in the dark, or his back to us.

- Remember that the Keystroke Killer resides in a fourth dimension and he can only interact with our world by taking the possession of a human being – Judas. You can include scenes in the fourth dimension or the possession of another body if Judas becomes too weak.

- You can write a brand new scene showing the murder of Matthew's sister, them as children in the park, or talking etc. Since she resides in the fourth dimension, she could "punch" her way to our dimension and try to make contact through an electronic device.

- Blaze can also try to "punch" through to our dimension and cry for help.

- You can have Blaze haunt Matthew (She becomes his conscience as his check and balance when she finally punches through to our dimension). This gives him hope to keep searching for his sister.

- Once someone has been "Deleted" by the Keystroke Killer, no one but Matthew remembers them. He holds the "Kryptonite" so speak or something is special about him that allows him to remember. The secret is he had a near-death experience and temporarily crossed over to the fourth dimension.

- Mag does or does not have to be included.

- New characters, returning or one-time appearance may be introduced.

- Matthew can develop a love interest.

- Matthew can have a partner.

- Each spec script must have another person *vanishing* as a result of the Keystroke Killer. This is what keeps Matthew in the game as a detective.

If a network, as a part of this series, produces your spec script, you will receive payment according to their payment schedule. I will get character as well as series creation credit. You will not be paid to submit a spec script and this announcement

in my book should in no way be misconstrued as an offering to appropriate or produce your screenplay. This is **not** an offer of employment, nor can I guarantee the production of your script. Moreover, On the Lot Productions, LLC, nor can I as the author of this book will be responsible for any liabilities involving coincidental similarities to works-in-progress or other submissions. The series is being shopped with Fox and the SciFy channel.

To find out how to submit your spec script, refer to the Appendix section on page 101 that provides the instructions on how to submit a script. Register your spec scripts with the WGA. Unregistered work will be tossed out and not read.

PRODUCING THE KEYSTROKE KILLER

I will also be looking for production crew all over the United States as I film different episodes. How do you get involved? Produce your version of *The Keystroke Killer* and show me what your team can do. Any filmmaker may use the screenplay *The Keystroke Killer,* included in this book, for **free** to produce a short film as long as you do three things:

1. Give me credit as the screenwriter and executive producer in the opening title credits, your website, on the DVD cover, poster, and on IMDB.

2. Invite me to set when you are filming at drmelcaudle@gmail.com. Who knows, you might get me as a free production assistant for the day. No promises, but if I'm available, it has happened before.

3. Send me a copy on a DVD of the completed film.

4. Please autograph it before sending it to me for my collection. Also, if you can, have your cast and crew autograph the cover of the screenplay. I'd like to have that as well because I collect autographed screenplays).

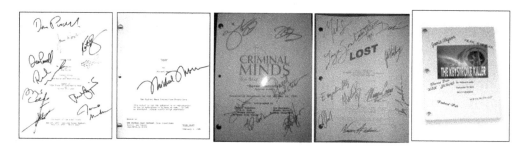

This is a great opportunity for your production team, e.g., director, director of photography, wardrobe, set designer, editor etc., to demonstrate their ability. Although you'll use the same screenplay, the results will vary because of diverse director's point of view as well as using a different crew, cast, props, set design, and locations. Each production holds the potential to be as unique as the cast and crew you assemble and the locations and wardrobes you choose.

Any profits you receive from selling your version of the film you keep as long as I get the aforementioned appropriate credit. If you need help with distribution, so you can recoup cost, you can sell it online at Create Space and Lulu.com. Distributing your video this way avoids any overhead costs, you maintain the rights to your own work (I still maintain screenwriter and creator rights), and you don't have the headaches of fulfilling orders. Another advantage is that the profit margin for you is more when you self-distribute. The downfall is you are responsible for all marketing for the film when you choose to self-distribute. The good news is *The Keystroke Killer* already has an audience and people clamor to watch different versions of the film as well as a fan base online.

What are you waiting for?

Take a chance and produce your version of *The Keystroke Killer*. It can be a lot of fun.

MY TURN

If you do decide to produce *The Keystroke Killer,* I will gladly give you free advice, and we can use Skype to communicate. That's just an option for you and is not mandatory. You can also visit www.onthelotproductions.com for character descriptions and their back-story as well as other information you can download for free to help you with your production. Free downloads include: sample call sheet, prop list, beat sheet, suggested shooting schedule etc. for *The Keystroke Killer*.

Once your version of the film is complete, I will announce it in my newsletter and send out an email blast to those on my social network sites and to my family and friends. I will also use my Facebook page and my Twitter account to tweet about it. If your production of *The Keystroke Killer* it is outstanding, I'll encourage you to submit it to film festivals and possibly consider your team for a future production for an On the Lot Productions, LLC feature film, short, or an episode for the television series *The Keystroke Killer*. I'll also link your production information of *The Keystroke Killer* to my production website if you want.

Take a chance and produce *The Keystroke Killer*. It can be a lot of fun for all of us.

THE KEYSTROKE KILLER FACEBOOK SITE

I have created a Facebook page for fans of *The Keystroke Killer*. Go there to discuss it with other readers and tell people about your version of the film.

@

THE KEYSTROKE KILLER FAN SITE

MERCHANDISE CENTER

By popular demand, coffee mugs, mouse pads, IPAD covers, T-shirts and more are available for purchase featuring the artwork and logo from *The Keystroke Killer*. Visit www.onthelotproductions.com to view the store.

PHOTOGRAPHY CREDITS

Numerous people have contributed photographs for the illustrations provided in this book. I cannot thank them enough for their contributions and I want to credit each of them. Likewise, www.freedigitalphotos.net provided photographs used with permission from the website.   I have taken every effort to ensure that each photographer or creator receives credit for his or her graphic design or photograph. I apologize in advance if I have made any errors. This was not my intent.

FRONT COVER DESIGN
Front Jacket Cover designed by Open Door Publishing House in conjunction with Dr. Mel Caudle

FRONT COVER FILMSTRIP TOP MONTAGE PHOTO CREDIT
Earth by XEDOS4 from Free Digital Photos
Taxi by Mantas Ruzveltas
Matthew's Sister's Grave Reflection – Cross-by TOPSTEP07 from Free Digital Photos and picture of young girl by Dr. Melissa Caudle – actor Jamie Alyson
Hollywood Hills Sign by On the Lot Productions, LLC
Race Car by Jon Whiles

FRONT COVER FILMSTRIP BOTTOM MONTAGE PHOTO CREDIT
Submarine photo by Robert Radford
Jamie Alyson by Dr. Melissa Caudle
Fire Fighters by Surachai
Fighter Jet by Tim Beach
Gun Shot by Steve Horder

BOOK COVERS FOR GUIDEBOOK SERIES PHOTO CREDIT
How to Write a Logline, Synopsis, and One Pager for Films and Reality TV designed by Open Door Publishing House in conjunction with Dr. Mel Caudle
How to Write a Logline: Quick Guidebook for Screenwriters designed by Open Door Publishing House in conjunction with Dr. Mel Caudle
How to Create a One Pager: Quick Guidebook for Screenwriters designed by Open Door Publishing House in conjunction with Dr. Mel Caudle
How to Write a Synopsis: Quick Guidebook for Screenwriters designed by Open Door Publishing House in conjunction with Dr. Mel Caudle

ACKNOWLEDGEMENT PHOTO CREDIT
Dr. Mel Caudle photo by Tim Moree

INTRODUCTION: THE MILLION-DOLLAR HOOK PHOTO CREDIT
Hook Montage created by On the Lot Productions, LLC
Aliens by Steve Maningham
Broadway Scripts by Michelle Rodriquez
Criss Angel by Dr. Melissa Caudle
Jamie Alyson by Hoda Hahn
Million Dollar Hook by Idea Go
Fighter Jet by Tim Beach
Firefighters by Nokhoog Buchachon
Wedding Couple on Beach by Kong Sky

FBI Agents provided by Michael Ardona

Earth with Keystroke Killer graphic created by On the Lot Productions, LLC – Earth photo by XEDOS4 from Free Digital Photos

How to Write a Logline, Synopsis, and One Pager for Films and Reality TV designed by Open Door Publishing House in conjunction with Dr. Mel Caudle

How to Write a Logline: Quick Guidebook for Screenwriters designed by Open Door Publishing House in conjunction with Dr. Mel Caudle

How to Create a One Pager: Quick Guidebook for Screenwriters designed by Open Door Publishing House in conjunction with Dr. Mel Caudle

How to Write a Synopsis: Quick Guidebook for Screenwriters designed by Open Door Publishing House in conjunction with Dr. Mel Caudle

The Keystroke Killer Screenplay Cover created by On the Lot Productions, LLC – Montage photo of Jamie Alyson by Hoda Hahn – Bloody Knife photo by Simon Howden

CHAPTER ONE – LOGLINES: THE HOOK PHOTO CREDIT

The Keystroke Killer Post Card created by On the Lot Productions, LLC – Bloody Knife in Sink photo by Simon Howden

The Other Man Screenplay Cover created by On the Lot Productions, LLC – Match Box photo by Carlos Porto

Diagram – Elements of a Logline created by On the Lot Productions, LLC

CHAPTER TWO – THE KEYSTROKE KILLER PHOTO CREDIT

The Keystroke Killer Post Card created by On the Lot Productions, LLC – Blood Splatter in photo by Simon Howden

Earth with *Keystroke Killer* graphic created by On the Lot Productions, LLC – Earth photo by XEDOS4 from Free Digital Photos

On the Lot Productions Logo created by Melanie Bledsoe

PG-13 Rating created by On the Lot Productions, LLC

The Keystroke Killer Screenplay Cover created by On the Lot Productions, LLC – Montage photo of Jamie Alyson by Hoda Hahn – Bloody Knife photo by Simon Howden

CHAPTER THREE – THE SUBJECT PHOTO CREDIT

Subject Cover Montage created by On the Lot Productions, LLC – all six photos of actor Jamie Alyson by Dr. Melissa Caudle with the exception of the lower middle photo by Hoda Hahn

Earth with *Keystroke Killer* Post Card graphic created by On the Lot Productions, LLC – Earth photo by XEDOS4 from Free Digital Photos

Question Mark graphic created by Digital Art

Blaze photo by Dr. Melissa Caudle – Actress Jamie Alyson

Matthew (Man) photo provided by Salvatore Vuono

Judas (Man at Computer) photo by Photo Stock

Mom and Tracy Blowing Bubbles by Castillo Dominici

Meg photo by Roger Molina – Model Kelly Rae

Jenni photo by Dr. Mel Caudle – actor Veronica Kelly

Landlord Reflection photo by Arvind Balaraman

Blaze at Lake photo by Dr. Mel Caudle – actor Jamie Alyson

The Keystroke Killer Screenplay Cover created by On the Lot Productions, LLC – Montage photo of Jamie Alyson by Hoda Hahn – Bloody Knife photo by Simon Howden

Matthew (Man) photo provided by Salvatore Vuono

Keyboard photo called Save Earth by Digital Art

Landlord Reflection photo by Arvind Balaraman

Who is Our Subject? Montage created by On the Lot Productions, LLC – photo of Eye Over Earth by Idea Go, Matthew (Man) photo provided by Salvatore Vuono, Blaze photo by Hoda Hahn – actor Jamie Alyson

CHAPTER FOUR – THE ACTION VERB PHOTO CREDIT
Action Montage created by On the Lot Productions, LLC, photos by the following photographers.
African Women Running by Africa from Free Digital Photos
Race Car by Jon Whiles
Criss Angel by Dr. Mel Caudle
Fantasia (Horse Warriors) by Dino De Luca
Gun Shot by Steve Horder
Fighter Jet by Tim Beach
Fire Fighters by Nokhoog Buchachon
Wedding Couple by Kong Sky
Hurricane by NASA
Fighter Jet by Tim Beach
Race Horses by Dino De Luca

CHAPTER FIVE – THE ACTION DESCRIPTION PHOTO CREDIT
Ticking by Kelly Peterson

CHAPTER SIX – THE OUTCOME PHOTO CREDIT
Metamorphosis by Graur Codrin
Blaze Checking Mail by On the Lot Productions, LLC – actor Jamie Alyson
Jennie and Blaze by Dr. Melissa Caudle – Actors Veronica Kelly and Jamie Alyson

CHAPTER SEVEN – ENHANCING LOGLINES PHOTO CREDIT
The Keystroke Killer Post Card created by On the Lot Productions, LLC – Blood Splatter in photo by Simon Howden
New Your City Skyline photo by Puttsky from Free Digital Photos
Farm House photo by Maggie Smith
Blaze as High School Graduate by Dr. Mel Caudle
Blaze in High Fashion by Hoda Hahn
Matthew's Sister's Grave Reflection – Cross-by TOPSTEP07 from Free Digital Photos and picture of young girl by Dr. Melissa Caudle – actor Jamie Alyson
Alter Ego, Raven, from the film *Demented Half* - written by Dr. Mel Caudle. Featured actor is Jamie Alyson.
Alter Ego, Angel, from the film *Demented Half* - written by Dr. Mel Caudle. Featured actor is Jamie Alyson.
Matthew (Man in Hood) photo provided by Salvatore Vuono
Matthew (Man Looking Away) photo provided by Salvatore Vuono
Matthew (Man Worried) photo provided by Salvatore Vuono
Matthew (Man Depressed) photo provided by Salvatore Vuono
On the Lot Productions, LLC Logo by Melanie Bledsoe

PHOTOGRAPHY SECTION PHOTO CREDIT
Dr. Mel on the set of *Dark Blue* photo by Tim Moree

ABOUT THE AUTHOR PHOTO CREDIT
Dr. Mel Caudle Portrait by Matthew Douglas

FOLLOW DR. MEL PHOTO CREDIT
Dr. Mel Caudle Portrait by Matthew Douglas

APPENDIX PHOTO CREDIT
How to Write a Logline, Synopsis, and One Pager for Films and Reality TV designed by Open Door Publishing House in conjunction with Dr. Mel Caudle
How to Write a Logline: Quick Guidebook for Screenwriters designed by Open Door Publishing House in conjunction with Dr. Mel Caudle

How to Create a One Pager: Quick Guidebook for Screenwriters designed by Open Door Publishing House in conjunction with Dr. Mel Caudle

How to Write a Synopsis: A Quick Guidebook for Screenwriters designed by Open Door Publishing House in conjunction with Dr. Mel Caudle

Writing Press Releases: Get Your Reality Show in the News designed by Open Door Publishing House in conjunction with Dr. Mel Caudle

Fundraising for Low-Budget Films designed by Open Door Publishing House in conjunction with Dr. Mel Caudle

The Film Production Coordinator designed by Open Door Publishing House in conjunction with Dr. Mel Caudle

How to Format a Reality Show designed by Open Door Publishing House in conjunction with Dr. Mel Caudle

The Art of the Production Coordinator: Impress for Success! designed by Open Door Publishing House in conjunction with Dr. Mel Caudle

The Reality of Reality TV: Reality Show Business Plans created by On the Lot Productions, LLC

The Reality of Reality TV: Workbook created by On the Lot Productions, LLC

The Reality of Reality TV: Reality Show Business Plans Template created by On the Lot Productions, LLC

150 Ways to Fund a Reality Show created by On the Lot Productions, LLC

Reality Show Handbook created by On the Lot Productions, LLC

The Reality Show Resource Logo created by On the Lot Productions, LLC

Dr. Mel Caudle portrait by Tim Moree

Dr. Mel, producer, on the set of the of her film *Dark Blue*

INDEX

fourth dimension, 62, 86

A

action description, 57, 58
Action verbs, 53
age. *See* logline enhancement,
antagonist, 47
apparitions, 62
ascension, 62

B

back-story, 63
Blaze, 47
business plan, 83

C

character arc, 59
character trait, 72, 74, *See*
    logline enhancement

D

desire. *See* logline
    enhancement
Diagram – Elements of a
    Logline, 15
**Do's and Don'ts of Logline
    Writing**, 83

E

emotional state. *See* logline
    enhancement
essential elements of a logline,
    13

F

fifth dimension, 62

G

Gladiator, 13

J

Judas. *Keystroke Killer*

L

lead characters, 47
location. *See* logline
    enhancement
logline, 7

M

Matthew, 47
Minority Report, 14
multiple subjects, 52
multi-sentence logline. *See*
    logline enhancement

N

name of a character. *See*
    logline enhancement
narrative plot, 46

O

outcome, 12, 13, 15, 48, 59, 60,
    63, 66, 67
Outcome of the Logline, 59

P

PG-13, 19

profession. *See* logline
    enhancement
protagonist, 9, 46, 47, 49, 51,
    52, 58
psychological thriller, 62

Q

quick reference guidebooks, 1

S

Subject of the Logline, 45
super power, 62

T

Template, 99
The Keystroke Killer, 2, 4, 6, 17,
    18, 38, 45, 46, 47, 48, 49, 51,
    52, 56, 58, 59, 60, 61, 62, 63,
    66, 67, 68, 69, 70, 71, 72, 73,
    75, 76, 78, 79, 80, 89, 92, 93,
    98
time travel, 62
transcendence, 21, 56, 61, 62,
    81, 83
transformation, 60

V

Verb of the Logline, 53

W

website, 91
Wizard of Oz, 14

ABOUT THE AUTHOR

Dr. Melissa Caudle earned a PhD in statistical research and administration from the University of New Orleans. She is a retired award winning high school principal who came into the television and film production arena in 1986 when she was on the morning news with a live episode talk-format segment dealing with educational issues for children. Capitalizing on her educational training and background, she uses her experience and training to bring her readers information that is easy to understand; yet, comprehensive. Her books for screenwriters, producers, and reality show creators are fast becoming the number one resources around the globe. Never before, has there been a more accomplished individual to share information. From her book *The Reality of Reality TV: Film Business Plans,* to her "how to books," Dr. Mel provides instruction and insight for her readers. She also published numerous books for screenwriters and reality show creators including *150 Ways to Fund a Reality Show*, *The Reality Show Handbook, Funding for Low-Budget Films,* and *How to Get Your Reality Show in the News.* Additional books are forthcoming in the winter of 2012 including the much-anticipated books *The Art of the Production Coordinator* and *The Film Production Travel Coordinator.*

Dr. Mel is also a feature and documentary filmmaker; including *Mexico Missions*, *The Dolphins in Terry Cove*, *The Alabama Gulf Coast Zoo*, *Sean Kelly's Irish Pub*, *Beauvoir,* and *Voices of the Innocent.* Her film credits include producer on the independent film *Dark Blue* and associate producer on the films *Varla Jean and the Mushroomheads* and *Girls Gone Gangsta.* Dr. Mel has worked on films such as the two Sony films, *STRAWDOGS* starring Kate Bosworth, James Marsden, and Alexander Skarsgard; *MARDI GRAS* starring Carmen Electra and Josh Gad; *On the Seventh Day* with Blair Underwood, Pam Grier, and Jamie Alyson; and *Dirty Politics* starring Melissa Peterman, Beau Bridges, and Judd Nelson. She also has been a program director for a television station in Alabama. Her company, On the Lot Productions, LLC is currently in pre-production on several feature films and reality show projects including River Kings. She has written 15 screenplays and created five reality shows. Dr. Mel currently lives in New Orleans, LA, is married, has three daughters, three sons-in-laws, and is the proud grandmother of three grandsons.

www.drmelcaudle.com

FOLLOW DR. MELISSA CAUDLE

Email: drmelcaudle@gmail.com

SOCIAL NETWORKING

Twitter: Melissa Caudle

Facebook: Melissa Ray Caudle

Facebook: The Reality of Reality TV

Facebook: The Keystroke Killer Fan Site

OFFICIAL WEBSITES

www.onthelotproductions.com

www.therealityofrealitytv.com

www.therealitytvresource.com

www.drmelcaudle.com

JOIN UP FOR DR. MEL'S FREE NEWSLETTER

WWW.THEREALITYOFREALITYTV.COM

BOOKS BY DR. MELISSA CAUDLE

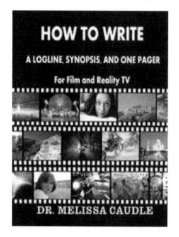

REALITY SHOW BOOKS

WWW.THEREALITYOFREALTYTV.COM

AVAILABLE ON AMAZON.COM

THE REALITY SHOW RESOURCE

www.therealitytvshowresource.com

If you want a listing on the links page, just ask for it. I'll be glad to approve a reciprocal link. While you are there, consider placing a small ad on the website to be seen thousands of times. As a reader of my book series, you get a special discount by telling me you purchased my book. Your discount code is RT-150FILM.

HOW TO SUBMIT A PROJECT

Many times, On the Lot Productions, LLC looks for a new film or reality show to produce. However, OTLP does not accept unsolicited screenplays or projects. The reason is to protect me as a producer, my production company, and you as a creator of a show or as a screenwriter. Many reality shows and screenplays resemble each other and we cannot be responsible if we already have a project similar to yours in production. To safeguard your project you must register it with the WGA and/or the U.S. Library of Congress for my company to consider. We will not consider any screenplay or reality show concept that does not include the registration number and those that aren't registered will immediately be destroyed and not read.

To submit a project to On the Lot Productions, LLC follow these steps:

1. Email our development producer at: OTLPdevelopment@gmail.com

2. In the subject line write, "Query on Film/Project – WGA # XXX)"

   If you are submitting an episode for *The Keystroke Killer* television series in the subject line write, "KSK SPEC SCRIPT."

3. Include in the body of the email, <u>attachments will not be opened,</u> the following information:

   - Registration number
   - Logline
   - Synopsis
   - Your contact information

If my development team is interested in your script or project, we will send you a submission agreement form. Story proposals and scripts arriving without the signed agreement or those that don't follow the procedures will be destroyed without review. A new query and/or agreement must be submitted with each new idea, proposal, or script and must be signed by all creators and copyright holders. Please note that On the Lot Productions, LLC and Dr. Melissa Caudle do not review unsolicited scripts, story ideas or any property not owned by the submitter. Such material will be destroyed without review. Do not send a screenplay or script without us asking you for it.

ANNOUNCING NEW PUBLICATION FROM OPEN DOOR PUBLISHING HOUSE

Check out the poem collection *Where the Mind Wanders,* written by Jamie Alyson, who is featured as Blaze in the cult classic *The Keystroke Killer.* Available from Amazon.com or www.opendoorpublishinghouse.com.

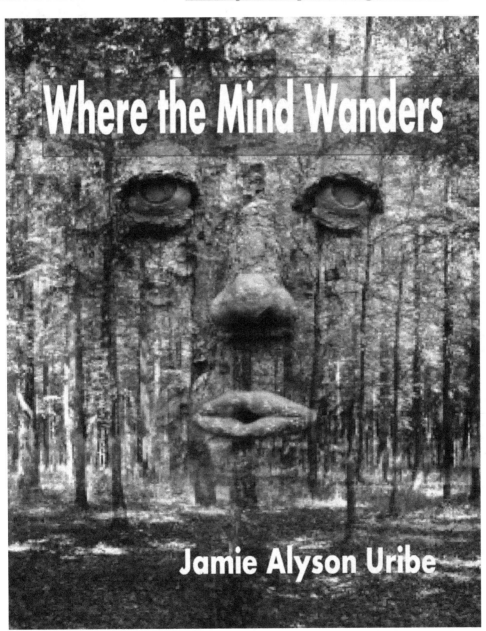

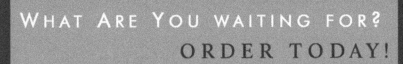

HOW TO CONTACT DR. MEL

To contact Dr. Mel for a speaking engagement, training, or production help in your area, email her at drmelcaudle@gmail.com or call 504- 264-1208.

To purchase her books go to www.onthelotproductions.com or purchase from Amazon.com.

Dr. Mel is also available for consultation to producers and screenwriters on creating your reality show, producting film or TV projects, and writing your screenplay.

www.onthelotproductions.com

NOW ACCEPTING
HEADSHOTS AND ACTOR REELS
The Keystroke Killer: Episode 1 - Transcendence
Do you want to be a part of the television Series?
Join the Facebook group to stay informed and for Casting call information etc.
THE KEYSTROKE KILLER FAN SITE
The casting directors from Los Angeles and New Orleans will use this site to scout actors. Upload your headshot and a demo reel. You may also suggest a character for a walk on role. Show us the who you want to be in a demo video. Upload a video. Let us see you!
Cast breakdown on the FILM PAGE of www.onthelotproductions.com

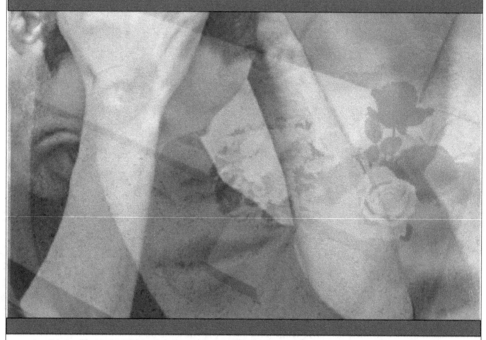

TRANSCENDENCE
Pilot Episode 1

THE KEYSTROKE KILLER

DR. MELISSA CAUDLE

CPSIA information can be obtained
at www.ICGtesting.com
Printed in the USA
LVHW060201070223
738864LV00017B/288

9 781467 993111